THE UNSPOKEN TRUTH
You Never Know Your Tomorrow

BY CHRISTABEL OPPONG

Copyright ©2025: Christabel Oppong

All rights reserved. No part of this publication may be produced, distributed, or transmitted in any form of by any means, including photocopying, recording, or other electronic or mechanical methods, without the prior written permission of the publisher, except in the case of brief quotations embodied in critical reviews and certain other non-commercial uses permitted by copyright law.

I have tried to recreate events, locales, and conversations from my memories of them. Some names and identifying details have been changed to protect the privacy of individuals.

First published in the United Kingdom, 2025
Published by Conscious Dreams Publishing
www.consciousdreamspublishing.com

Cover Designer: Anze Ban
Editor: Rhoda Molife, Molah Media
Proofreader: Daniella Blechner
Typesetter: Amit Dey

ISBN 978-1-917584-70-8

DEDICATION

For my parents, Mr Francis and Mrs Agnes Oppong, whose lives, struggles and love shaped every word of this book. May your spirits find peace and your truths never be forgotten.

ACKNOWLEDGEMENTS

This book is born out of love, pain and truth, and it stands as a tribute to my late parents. Their strength, their struggles and their humanity have shaped not only this story but the person I've become.

To my brother Elvis, thank you for standing by me through life's challenges. Our shared memories and mutual respect mean more than words can say.

To my three children, Jermaine, Briana and Amari, you are my greatest blessing. Your patience, understanding and unconditional love gave me the courage to finish this book when it felt too heavy to continue. You remind me every day why truth and compassion matter.

To my cousin Priscilla and extended family who offered encouragement and understanding, thank you for holding space for my grief and my growth.

I am also grateful to the dedicated team at Conscious Dreams Publishing, Daniella Blechner and Rhoda Molife, for guiding me through each stage of this process with professionalism and care.

Thank you to Anze Ban for the amazing book cover.

Finally, to every reader who finds a part of their own story in these pages, may this book remind you that even through injustice, loss and heartache, there is always room for healing ... and hope.
Christabel

INTRODUCTION

It was a rainy morning in June, and I was visiting my father. He called me into his room where he was lying in bed.

"I wish you'd stay longer," he said in a croaky voice.

I stepped into the dimly lit room, the only light coming from his bedside lamp. He strained to give me his familiar bright smile, then tried to sit up, his hands resting on the blanket that was covering his lap. He looked almost regal, with his full head of salt-and-pepper hair. Blinking back the unexpected tears, I silently put a hand on his arm as I stood next to him.

"The kids are growing up well," he said, looking into my eyes and holding my gaze.

He recounted how the oldest of the grandchildren, my son, had tried to play a magic trick on him, throwing a coin in the air and making it 'disappear' by dropping it a few feet behind him. We shared a quiet laugh, the corners of Dad's eyes crinkling in amusement.

"I see so much of myself in that boy," he said.

My heart grew warm as I nodded. Pride puffed my shoulders, knowing that this compliment was a milestone. It made me realise how far we'd come. Having watched him grow to love my little boy in stages, to hear him now say this was wonderful. To the outside world, Francis Oppong seemed very reserved. What many of them didn't know was that it was hard for him to trust people, the result of having been locked up and tortured as a young man.

"People can't be trusted," he'd always say.

And as I unravelled his life story, I began to understand why he thought that.

"You can befriend them, but don't trust them! People can be backstabbers, standing right behind you and promising to catch you if you fall, only to go after their selfish interests once they have an opportunity to do so."

Although he projected a reserved front to the public, those who knew him found him to be a jovial person who especially loved joking around with his kids and grandchildren. I never went for more than three days without speaking to him. Then when I did, he was as cheerful as ever. He enjoyed discussing the past, and as always, I eagerly listened to his stories. He was a masterful storyteller, even holding my interest when he told the same story twice because there was a twist to it every time. Yet when I looked into his dark eyes, I always saw the hurt and pain as he shared his life story with me again and again.

"You need to write a book about my life," he would often say to me.

Now is the time for me to do so, because in this life, you never know your tomorrow.

1

Francis Oppong was worried. He was newly married, but the catastrophe Ghana had become was no longer a place to raise a child. Many years before, as a teen, he'd left his hometown to pursue his chosen career, and now one of the men who had meant so much to him was gone forever. Francis felt nothing but guilt about having abandoned him. He wished he hadn't been so hard-headed as a youth and had just followed a simple path. At the same time, he also knew that it was now too late for such regrets because the hands of time could not be turned back. All he could hope for was that his choices today wouldn't leave him with additional regrets tomorrow.

His country was well versed in regret. Since independence in 1957, Ghana had seen a succession of flawed leaders who'd consistently worsened the mess left behind by their predecessors. The current one, Jerry Rawlings, had promised so much at the beginning, yet he was now on track to lead the nation towards economic ruin. Just like the other Ghanaian presidents and military leaders before him, he quelled any unrest and coup attempts by jailing opposition leaders. Francis had been fiercely supportive of Rawlings at the start, and his loyalty had been rewarded with a couple of promotions to senior roles. However, doubts about this new Ghanaian government, a military junta, had crept in as he'd witnessed the country's decline.

Out of the blue though, came an escape route: two of his sisters-in-law had invited him and his wife to visit them in the UK. With the current state of affairs at home, and no way forward in sight, Francis was excited about the trip, fully aware that 'a visit' could swiftly turn into a permanent move if everything worked out well. But did he really want that? Regardless of the chaos in Ghana, Francis wasn't one to run from his problems. He never wanted to be in a position again where he'd feel guilty about abandoning someone or, someplace, he loved.

What would I even do in the UK? he wondered. After all, while he had considerable power in Ghana, he had no advanced education, and certainly no transferrable skills that would be welcomed in a different country.

Francis had always dreamed of using his power to create a better Ghana. Now though, he felt like he would have done better without those dreams because his country was slowly dying. The disheartening truth was that at this juncture in his life and that of the nation, he would end up regretting it if he left, just as much as he would if he stayed. Contemplating this indisputable fact, there and then, Francis made up his mind about what he had to do.

* * *

It was late one evening in mid-July, the rainy season in Ghana, and every member of the Oppong family lay awake awaiting the arrival of a new baby. Yaw Oppong, having experienced this scenario 11 times already, wasn't as relaxed and unconcerned as one might have expected. He paced the hell out of his already worn footwear while biting his short nails down to the cuticle, willing the midwife to emerge from the bedroom with good news. In fact, the sound of a crying baby would have sufficed, but for now, there was nothing.

It turned out that this particular birth wasn't exactly a smooth one, which was very different from the previous that had happened so quickly. This time, Yaw ended up anxiously walking around their small house in a rural village for four days. Finally, on 24 July 1958, in the middle of a stormy night, the midwife emerged, beads of sweat on her smiling face as she opened her mouth to make an announcement. Yaw didn't wait for the words as her smile was all the answer he needed. Kneeling on the floor, he bowed his head to his Creator. Then, with a slight nod towards the midwife, he bundled past her and burst into the bedroom to see his child.

He cried out in joy at the sight of his eighth son, lithe and dark with a tiny head full of dark, short curls. Yaw was the proudest father ever, so proud in fact, that one would've thought he'd pushed the baby out himself. Those few days of restless waiting had done nothing to dim his happiness as he danced around the bedroom and hailed his wife for giving birth to yet another boy, thereby adding to the family line.

"You're the strongest woman in the world," he said. "A woman after my own heart."

Outside, the heavens shook, and lightning streaked across the night sky every few minutes. The wind rattled the windows, threatening to pull them off their hinges and making the dark curtains dance as if possessed. The very foundations of the house trembled, and some drops of rain dripped into the room, which was lit by a single bulb dangling precariously from the white ceiling. In the midst of all this, the midwife gingerly wrapped the newborn in a colourful blanket and gave the mother a meaningful glance that said, 'This will do. No more.'

Afia Agyeiwaa lay on the thin mattress, exhausted. She watched her husband dance around the room and then managed a small nod towards the midwife while stretching her arms out to take her baby son. She smiled down at the tiny being she'd carried in her stomach for nine months. Until a few minutes ago, she'd thought that neither of them would make it. Her fear had stayed with her until she'd heard the first cry of the baby; and even then, she hadn't been sure if he'd survive. Looking at his face now, though, Afia could tell that he was a strong little man. The fact that she'd successfully brought him into the world against all odds gave her a great sense of satisfaction too. She felt a genuine sense of value; she'd done her husband proud. Equally, she was determined that this son would be the last of their 12 children.

* * *

Yaw didn't spare a penny for the naming ceremony because he knew what it meant to have his wife and baby healthy and strong, considering the circumstances surrounding the boy's birth. He invited his extended family for the event and insisted that they all present a name for the newborn. Yet, as he stood there watching the child being passed from one family member to another, he couldn't help but feel a sense of dread because he realised that he hadn't decided on a name himself. He'd done this 11 times already, so there was no excuse for forgetting that his son would need a name. He also knew that Afia would feel hurt if he admitted that he hadn't thought of one. So, he kept his frustrations to himself and simply watched quietly as one name after another was called out by their relatives as well as some of his friends who were also in attendance.

"So, what's your choice?" Afia eventually asked him.

Yaw hesitated. "I want it to be a surprise," he said.

As he stood in the centre among the familiar faces gathered around him, his baby son cradled securely in his arms, his youngest sister's hand shot up.

"I still haven't given you my name for him yet," she said.

Seeing this as an opportunity to save face, Yaw waited for her to speak.

"Francis," she said in a quiet voice.

Yaw smiled broadly and nodded. "That's the name I've chosen too," he said. "This must be destiny."

Later that night, when everyone was gone and he and Afia went to sleep on the thin mattress where she'd given birth, he told her the truth about not having had a name for the baby. Afia recognised the humour in the situation, so they shared a quiet laugh.

Like his siblings, the baby boy, whose full name was Francis Oppong, was raised a Muslim. His parents were not wealthy at all, but they managed to provide for all their kids. Indeed, the Oppong men prided themselves on single-handedly looking after their respective families, a trait that Yaw would instil in his eight sons. Yaw was a herbalist and a hard-working man. He went on daily trips to the outskirts of the village to sell his herbal medicines, while at other times, he spent days away from home to find and study new herbs to potentially add to his offering. Even as the modern world developed in the second half of the 20th century, he didn't care if people looked down on him because of his traditional occupation.

"To survive, there is no shame," he often said.

He packaged his medicines so well you wondered if he'd graduated from some prestigious school of business, which of course, wasn't the case. In fact, Yaw had never even been to school. He was illiterate, but more importantly, he was intelligent and wise. He called his wisdom 'costly sense', having acquired it the hard way, through experience peppered with a few hard knocks. As a result, he encouraged his children to learn from him.

Since his herbs were very effective, Yaw was well respected and popular in his village. His medicines healed people with various illnesses and helped women in the village to conceive. Although he had lots of customers from far and wide, the herbal business wasn't exactly oil money. Even if it had been, it still wouldn't have amounted to much, for Yaw was a man who was far too kind, selling most of his medicines at little to no cost in a bid to help as many people as possible.

Like most African women, Afia was a homemaker, taking care of the kids and cooking delicious meals for the entire family. It was a role she embraced with pride but was no less gruelling than the work done by paid labourers in the fields and on construction sites. It was a role only a mother could do and do well. With some of the older boys and girls already grown, Afia's workload had remained steady over the years despite the arrival of more babies. Each child was responsible for a routine task in the household, as Afia knew that this was the best way to raise children into responsible adults.

Growing up, Francis was neither a mummy's nor a daddy's boy; he loved both his parents very much and aimed to please them by being obedient. He reserved his obedience only for them, though. As is common with the youngest child in the family, Francis was very spoiled. His parents indulged him without remorse, and he got away with literally everything, especially when he claimed his siblings' things as his own. By the time Francis was six, he would often show off his supposed new toy to his parents in the mornings only for an older brother or sister to claim ownership of it. Francis didn't care about the truth of the matter. Instead, he'd run to his mother, who would protect him from his frustrated siblings.

Thus, he learnt at an early age to take and claim things without having to beg for them. Sharp-eyed and a fast runner, his thin legs would carry him around the house as he escaped a telling of, or worse, a beating from his siblings. Soon, they nicknamed him 'the house terror'. Even when their mother warned them to stop using the name, it stuck and remained Francis's moniker throughout his childhood and his early teens.

Despite his stubbornness, Francis was very good at school and top of his class. He was so bookish and academically gifted that some of his teachers would come to the house to tell Yaw about his outstanding contributions in class. Of course, this made Yaw very proud, and in turn, he would boast to his friends about his youngest son.

Aside from being very close to his parents, Francis developed a strong bond with his older brothers, especially the eldest of the 12 children, George Arthur. George was already an adult by the time Francis was born and basically helped to raise him. Whenever their parents were busy, George would take care of Francis, making sure that he wasn't bullied by the rest of the siblings and maintaining the peace amongst them.

Yaw was a very religious man and considered it a sacrilege to miss the Jumu'ah - the Friday prayer. Regardless of what he was doing or where he was, he always went to the mosque and prayed during the prayer hours. He tried to instil this habit in his children too. Of course, kids being kids, the Oppong brood didn't necessarily follow his example, and the fact that Afia wasn't as devoted made it even worse. However, Francis felt very differently about the Jumu'ah prayers. He would follow his dad to the mosque even on those Fridays when the rest of the family didn't feel compelled to. In fact, he went with his father almost everywhere, revelling in the fact that this enabled him to leave the house and get away from his siblings. He was particularly keen to escape from his sister Akua Biaa, who seemed to detest his very existence and always found ways to attack him.

Absolutely no one fascinated Francis as much as his dad did. On those lone trips with him, in search of herbs or to sell more medicines, the boy learnt a lot of lessons that stuck with him for the rest of his life. Yaw was in awe of nature and explained all his research to little Francis, who at just ten years old, was already able to brag about cooking up herbal medicines for different ailments. Since his dad also allowed him to administer them, their patients were invariably wowed to be treated by a mere child, filling Yaw with pride.

From a tender age, Francis's head was firmly screwed on, and he wholeheartedly looked forward to having his own herbal-medicine business when he grew up.

However, he was determined to earn more than his father and understood that to achieve this, he wouldn't be able to charge as little as Yaw did, let alone give medicines away for free. Francis was eager to turn his craft into a money-making machine. His innocent view of medication as a means to an end received a sudden reality check when he was 13 years old. That was when he witnessed one of Yaw's patients die from strange complications of either the illness or medication. In fact, Francis watched the old man take his last breath, which was the first time he had seen somebody die. What he didn't know then was that it would be the last time.

Rumours started to spread in the community that Yaw's herbs had killed the man, even though there was no proof to support this allegation. Unsurprisingly, the Oppongs were terrified, fearing that their livelihood was at risk. Meanwhile, the patient's death had left young Francis shell-shocked, and he started asking himself some profound questions. Were herbal medicines truly the panacea he'd believed them to be? And more importantly, were they really going to provide a prosperous future for him?

His perspective changed when the realisation hit him that the answers to both questions were 'no'. Clearly, even the herbs his beloved father researched and gathered with great care couldn't cure every ailment in the world, and sometimes, they failed altogether. This wasn't a risk that Francis was prepared to take for his own life; failure was not an option. So, he turned his back on herbal medicine and started searching for a new path towards securing his future.

2

When Yaw's patient passed away, it had shaken Francis to his core, convincing him that medicine could not provide the certainty he longed for. At the same time, his country too was teetering on the edge of uncertainty. In early 1972, Ghana was restless, its army restless too, and Francis was about to witness how fragile governments could be. The First Lady of the United States, Pat Nixon, wife of the then-president Richard Nixon, unwittingly prevented a military coup in Ghana. In January 1972, six months after Francis Oppong had turned 13, she became the first wife of a sitting American President to visit Africa, travelling to Liberia, Cote d'Ivoire and Ghana over the course of eight days. In the Oppongs' home country, she danced with local people and addressed the Parliament, unaware, like everybody else, that Colonel Ignatius Kutu Acheampong, then Commander of Ghana's First Infantry Brigade, and his allies had been planning to overthrow the government precisely on that day, 6 January 1972; the colonel had been leading the brigade since 1968. Yet because of Pat Nixon's visit, they decided to postpone their plans and instead seized control exactly a week later.

By then, Ghana had existed as an independent country for 15 years, having been created in 1957 by combining the territories of two British Crown Colonies (Ashanti and the Gold Coast Colony), a British Protectorate (the Northern Territories of the Gold Coast) and a United Nations Trust Territory (British Togoland). The new nation was a republic, but in name only as Ghana's first President, Kwame Nkrumah, had run an authoritarian government, which in turn had been violently deposed and replaced by a succession of military rulers. In 1969, Kofi Busia, a former Oxford University Fellow and Professor of Sociology and Culture of Africa at a Dutch university, had restored civilian leadership for the first time in several years. However, on 13 January 1972, Acheampong's bloodless coup d'état once more established a military government.

As someone whose main interests in life included helping others and appreciating nature for both its beauty and the remedies it provided, Yaw Oppong viewed politicians and the military with suspicion. He knew that many of his fellow Ghanaians were out of work and struggled with the sharp rise in food prices as economic mismanagement and arbitrary arrests (both of which had defined even Professor Busia's time in office) haunted ordinary citizens. If nothing else, Yaw therefore wanted his children to be wary of those who ruled their country, fully aware by this stage in his life that powerful people all too often abused the privileges they enjoyed.

It was an outlook on life that had been shaped by the historic changes in Ghana over the years since independence. It also stood in sharp contrast to the naivety of his youngest son, who, after renouncing herbal medicine, started to develop a fascination with the one thing his father wanted him to steer clear of: the military. Perhaps it was the fact that soldiers were able to blend into the natural environment Yaw had taught him to cherish, camouflaged as they were in their green uniforms. More likely though, it was their weapons that impressed Francis, who just like most boys his age, liked to play with toy guns. He was in awe of the men as they marched up and down the village, proudly wielding their firearms as if they had in fact been born with them. The sense of duty they exuded and their appearance piqued his interest so much that he wanted to find out more about them and their work.

The men in green were all Francis talked about now - to his friends, his siblings and anybody else who would listen. His curiosity came with a lot of questions, which he posed to his dad. But Yaw froze upon seeing his son's enthusiasm and made his opinion on the matter clear.

"Francis. You don't want to get involved with the military," he'd say.

At the time, Francis didn't understand what his father meant, or rather, he didn't care to know. Instead, there and then, he decided that he wanted to join the army one day. Young and rebellious at heart, he was too intrigued by the soldiers to have his ambitions shattered by mere words. If anything, the fact that those big guns were, as far as Yaw was concerned, supposed to be out of reach made them look even more appealing. Francis badly wanted to wield one, so he started making toy rifles out of sticks that he found on his many walks in the bush with his dad. Then he would hide in the expanse of empty land at the back of their house and practise marching among the shrubs while brandishing his 'weapons' like he'd seen the soldiers do.

* * *

Over the next couple of years, Francis regularly sneaked out of the house or stayed back after school to polish his 'army skills'. For this reason, he'd often miss out on playing with his siblings and friends and would even skip meals. This took a chunk out of him, so much so that his mother soon noticed how thin and withdrawn he was.

"What's wrong, Francis?" she would worriedly ask him.

But Francis would just shrug and say nothing.

"He's becoming a man," Yaw would say to Afia, which would invariably be the end of the discussion.

By the time he was 15, most of Francis's siblings had left the family home and lived on their own. His four sisters were married. Some of his brothers who had fallen into the habit of late nights and staying away for several days at times were eventually practically chased out of the house by Yaw. His reasoning was that they'd be better off not returning at all. For Francis, the home he'd grown up in soon felt empty and abandoned, and quite frankly, he couldn't stand it. He began to slowly lose his mind, spending more and more time playing soldier and wishing he was old enough to strike out on his own. He envied his siblings for leaving their parental home and hated them for abandoning him. All he could focus on was how and when he'd eventually become a soldier, somebody who was feared and respected.

* * *

When he eventually shared his dream for the future with his mother, she was aghast, recounting several stories about soldiers being heartless.

"They kill by guns, and they'd be willing to die by guns," she warned him.

Although those words would stick with Francis, his mind was made up since he saw things differently. Painfully aware of the turmoil Ghana had undergone throughout his short lifetime, when he fantasised about wielding power and a gun, he envisioned himself helping the masses and making positive changes. In a sense, to him, being a soldier felt like administering herbal medicine to the sick.

"I'll be fine," he therefore told his mother, and ignoring the tears that filled her eyes, he stomped out of the room.

Nothing could stop him, not even his father's stern rebuke and threat to disown him if he went ahead with his plan to join the military. By this point, Francis was living and breathing the idea, so it mattered not what his father thought. He loved the thought of becoming a soldier and had already put all his energy into this newfound path; it was too late to back out now because he couldn't imagine himself doing anything else.

His parents made no attempt to hide their intense displeasure with his choice of career. This made life at home very uncomfortable for Francis. Yet he knew that he had to do what was right for him. As a result, there were lots of arguments between him and his parents, as well as some of his siblings. However, a few of them were inclined to take his side, though they couldn't openly voice their opinions for fear of their father's wrath.

Seeing the army as a path to certain death, Yaw remained adamant that Francis should become a herbalist like him. In fact, he was greatly looking forward to them working together once the boy became an adult as he valued his intelligence and the knowledge of herbal medicine he'd already gained. Being the head of the family, it was totally out of the question for Yaw that his youngest son wouldn't follow his wishes. However, Yaw was a practical man and facing the reality of the situation, however shocking, he began to fast and pray to avert disaster.

To be fair, for a long time, Francis had thought he was destined to emulate his father and succeed him in the herbal trade, yet a change had come in the twinkle of an eye. Despite his strong conviction that he needed to do what was best for him, he still felt like a traitor, and it was difficult for him to move past the heavy burden of going against his dad. However, as time passed, he reached a point where he wasn't exactly sorry anymore. Instead, he began to think about a lot of things. He had 11 healthy siblings, yet none had followed in their father's footsteps; every single one of them had chosen their own path. So, Francis couldn't understand why he had to be the one who had to bear his cross and take up the family trade.

One day, he posed that question to his dad. But Yaw just gave him a sad look, then shook his head.

"Have you gone insane?" Yaw asked his son in disbelief.

From that moment onwards, the house became a prison for Francis. In fact, he began to feel caged even when he walked the streets of their village at night. He couldn't shake off the feeling of being held down by his parents. He was now at the stage where he frequently thought about how it would feel to have a gun in his hand and the right to shoot. The excitement of the power, the authority that only the army could give him felt like an intoxicating drug. He was addicted and so it would have to be the military or nothing at all.

One day in late 1973, now aged 15, Francis left Mampong Secondary School after his last lesson and without informing his parents, went to the local barracks and boldly walked in. He was accompanied by an older friend who was intrigued by his strong conviction to join the army, and by the fact that he was willing to go as far as disobeying his parents to do so; that boldness had given him the courage to do the same. They strode in together, filled out the recruitment forms and waited in the long queue of healthy, strong young men who were eager to serve their nation.

However, the recruitment test scared Francis so much that he began to think about waiting another year before enlisting. He was the right height, not married and had obtained the required credits in core English. The thing was, he had long been mocked by his peers for his slight frame, and those voices echoed in his mind as he stood among the sturdier boys. He was sure that his weight wouldn't meet the minimum threshold, meaning that he would not qualify.

Yet when the results came, it was his friend who got disqualified on account of alcohol dependency. Francis was very surprised to hear that because he'd never seen him drink; apparently, the military had snuffed him out on the urine test. Meanwhile, Francis had made it in, seemingly by sheer luck. His excitement knew no bounds and that evening, his friend (who remained nonchalant about getting rejected) took him to a bar for the first time to celebrate. Francis went home drunk that night.

His seismic decision to visit the barracks that afternoon would go down as his first major act of disobedience towards his parents. Yet when he told them the news, just about managing to appear his usual sober self, they wished him well, albeit reluctantly.

"Come back home if it gets too tough," his mum said, her eyes red from crying.

3

As it inevitably turned out, the army training wasn't what Francis had anticipated it to be. Those practice sessions with sticks for guns were no substitute for the real thing, and getting woken up at 3am by an angry drill instructor screaming in his face was the least of his problems.

The training programme focused on intense drilling, weapons handling, physical fitness and first aid. It wasn't for the faint-hearted and Francis realised with a sense of dread that he had two options: either make it or return home, tail between his legs and face being mocked by all and sundry. That was if he made it out of the camp alive, which seemed increasingly unlikely as minutes turned into hours on his first day.

Growing up in a large family, Francis was used to being told what to do. But he knew that he could get away with disobeying his parents and siblings, or at least he was able to complain about what they asked him to do. By contrast, in the military, he was told when to eat, when to sleep, when to wake and when to use the toilet. Moreover, he was expected to accept these instructions without so much as a murmur. It was pure mind control and if he dared to question the orders of his superiors, he would not just get thrown out of the army, he could actually end up in jail.

For the first time, Francis began to understand his dad's frustration about his plan to become a soldier, and the stark fear he'd seen in his mother's eyes. The military wasn't a place for civilians like him; it was hell. The instructors weren't simply eager to drum the military way into him — they also wanted to beat the crap out of him before the army spent too much money on his training. Francis started to grasp this concept as he contemplated the activities that were used to break him and his fellow recruits. The rigid routine and absolute control over every aspect of his life was tough, but it turned out that he was even tougher. He'd taken a plunge into the unknown when he'd decided to turn his back on his parents and join the army, and he was determined to see it through no matter what.

He made a few friends but soon realised that keeping up friendships in the military was difficult, especially after he watched a comrade collapse during one of the strenuous drills on the barracks field and die on the spot. Meanwhile, a bunkmate took ill and also never recovered. The thought of losing his life kept Francis up at night as he worried about failing before he could even get started. In his mind, failing was for weaklings, and the Oppongs weren't weaklings ... well at least not Francis Oppong, anyway.

Unsurprisingly, weapons handling was his favourite exercise given that it had been this very aspect of the men in green that had captured his imagination. He excelled at it to the point that one of the instructors noticed and nicknamed him 'Gunner'. Francis loved first aid, too. Having spent more than half his life administering medicines to people, it was easy for him to excel here too. Having these two critical skills under his belt somewhat elevated Francis in the eyes of his instructors, who subsequently found less reason to bark in his face.

In January 1974, Francis completed his initial training in the army camp and was posted to the 3rd Battalion Infantry in Sunyani, the capital of central Ghana's Brong-Ahafo region. By now he'd become used to the harsh military environment and so ended up staying with the battalion for several years. During that period, the 3rd Infantry frequently supported United Nations troops to keep the peace in the Congo, where a political crisis in the first half of the '60s had destabilised not just the country but all of Central Africa. These tours of duty, as well as being stationed in a different part of Ghana, meant that Francis couldn't see his family and soon lost touch with them. Yet serving on the frontline also enabled him to grow up and change to the point that life as a soldier became his true identity.

* * *

Having distinguished himself in the army, in 1978, Francis was sent on a six-week course for Junior Non-commissioned Officers to learn about jungle tactics and warfare. The humidity and dense vegetation of Ghana's rainforest made for a challenging environment, often restricting one's field of vision to 20 feet or less. This also provided ample opportunity for camouflage and the development of innovative military strategies, while the forest offered plenty of materials to build fortifications.

However, the terrain was largely inaccessible to vehicles which made it hard to deliver transportation and supplies. In turn, air travel became just as important as medical services, which were in constant demand due to the harsh environment, with soldiers suffering from various tropical diseases. In fact, Francis had to helplessly look on again as one of his comrades succumbed to a virus and died. Fighting two enemies, man and nature, was a huge challenge. Somehow though, Francis managed to cling on to his health as others suffered or perished.

Then one day, he was sent on a field training exercise on a shoreline fringed with mangrove trees that were almost impenetrable. Beads of sweat on his face, he was advancing on his own through the swamp under the midday sun, his colleagues having been dropped off in another part of the dense forest. As he slowly and quietly pressed ahead in the suffocating heat, Francis suddenly felt a sharp pain in his ankle. It was a snake bite. When he saw the perfectly camouflaged reptile, he cried out in both shock and pain, and as the snake slithered off into the thick vegetation, he almost immediately felt drowsy.

Sitting down in the mud next to a tree, Francis considered what to do, but he couldn't think straight, his mind foggy. Hoping against hope that he was merely suffering from exhaustion due to the intense heat, he grabbed his water bottle from his rucksack with shaking hands. Rehydrating didn't make him feel any better and the realisation hit him that the snake had been a venomous one.

None of his comrades were nearby and Francis could feel himself getting weaker and weaker at an alarming speed. He tried to call out for his colleagues, but his voice was by then raspy and barely audible; there was no way they would have heard him, even if they'd been just a few feet away. Plus, even if they'd got him onto a plane and out of the jungle right away, it probably would have been too late as his strength was fading fast. Francis was certain that the end had come. Then, he suddenly felt bloated, a known effect of the venom. To make matters worse, a storm appeared on the horizon and quickly engulfed the mangrove forest. In response, he just shut his eyes and willed his life away.

Suddenly, as he drifted off, he felt a slap in the face and woke up. Opening his eyes, he saw the anxious wet face of his commandant right above him in the pouring rain. Then everything became a blur.

* * *

Somehow, his commandant and fellow officers must have managed to drag Francis back to their camp. The storm went on to last for several days, but it didn't stop the 3rd

Infantry from training, meaning that they had to leave him behind to recuperate in a leaky makeshift tent. Stuck there, Francis felt useless and incredibly lonely. He was far away from home, in the heart of the hostile environment of the jungle. Feeling close to death, his life flashed before his eyes and he realised how much he missed his parents and siblings. The truth was that it wasn't just the physical distance that had caused him to drift away from them; he'd deliberately avoided his family since joining the army. Now, for the first time in five years, he just wanted to go home. He couldn't wait to get out of the jungle, if he stayed alive long enough to do so.

Fortunately, by virtue of his young age of 20 years, Francis recovered within a few weeks, though the first few days were spent confined to his bunk, his leg swollen and throbbing with pain, while the distant sounds of training echoed outside. He remained in camp throughout, watched closely by his comrades until he was strong enough to return to training. As his health was restored, his new identity as a soldier also returned, prompting him to put his plans to see his family on hold again. In fact, there was no time for him to visit them anyway as Ghana's continued political turmoil meant that the army was constantly on high alert.

By the summer of 1978, Colonel Acheampong was still leading the country, but there was widespread discontent with his government, which was accused of corruption while ordinary citizens suffered due to soaring food prices. Ironically, after having come to power via a coup, Acheampong went on to be ousted in another military uprising led by Lieutenant General Fred Akuffo in July 1978, a senior army officer who had risen through the ranks to become Chief of Defence Staff. However, ten months later, on the 15th of May 1979, Akuffo himself faced a coup staged by 31-year-old Flight Lieutenant Jerry Rawlings, an ambitious young soldier who had joined the air force at the age of 23; he and other soldiers who were unhappy about not receiving their salaries.

However, the insurrection was quashed. The soldiers were put on trial, during which Rawlings severely criticised Akuffo's government. Unsurprisingly, he was sentenced to death. However, just a couple of weeks later, on the night of 3 June, some junior military officers broke into his jail and freed him. The following day, in events that would become known as the June 4th Revolution, Rawlings and his allies rounded up their superiors, including Akuffo and Acheampong, as well as another former head of state, Akwasi Afrifa. All three of them were executed by firing squads later that month. Meanwhile, Rawlings was installed to run the country until the scheduled presidential elections later that year.

Being a junior military officer too, Francis took an active part in the June 4th uprising. While the revolution was welcomed by many, its immediate aftermath gave rise to terrible atrocities as some soldiers, driven by a desire to punish corrupt officials, went on a rampage. Under the infamous slogan 'Let the blood flow', there was a total breakdown of law and order, with arbitrary arrests, beatings, abductions and killings. Countless entrepreneurs were also targeted and had their assets seized, with students cheering as generals were shot and traders humiliated. So, although the 4th of June became a notable day in Ghana's history, it was also a date that brought a lot of pain to many people who either lost loved ones, businesses or had to flee the country. Nevertheless, the presidential elections went ahead, and as things quietened down, Rawlings peacefully handed over his power to the politician and former diplomat Hilla Limann in September 1979. Still, during this time of upheaval, nothing ever seemed certain or permanent.

For Francis, change was to come again a couple of years later, in June 1981, when his battalion left the turmoil at home behind to support the United Nations Interim Force in Lebanon (UNIFIL) for six months. Three years earlier, in March 1978, Israel had avenged a terrorist attack near Tel Aviv by invading southern Lebanon. This had prompted the UN to establish its peacekeeping mission via UNIFIL to defuse the hostilities and ensure Israel's withdrawal from its northern neighbour. Another goal was to help restore normal economic and social life in the region by upgrading roads, water and electricity supplies, as well as health and education services.

Francis and his troops were deployed in the eastern part of the central sector, whose headquarters were in the small town of Kfar Dounin. Their accommodation was supposedly warm enough for the harsh Lebanese winter, but by the time they arrived, protective walls made of various bullet- and shock-resistant materials were still being erected around the buildings to increase the soldiers' safety. Their water supply was also inadequate. Meanwhile, restrictions on petrol consumption caused problems that were compounded by the fact that many of the available vehicles were over 20 years old and in serious need of repairs. Taking it all in, Francis once more wondered why he'd taken such a difficult path in his life.

On 28 June 1981, UNIFIL's Deputy Chief of Staff was ambushed by an armed group while travelling across southern Lebanon. The escort vehicle was hit and one Ghanaian soldier was injured. An investigation was launched, but the group responsible for the incident was not identified.

A few weeks later, in mid-July, there was a serious outbreak of hostilities in areas outside UNIFIL control, which prompted many people there to escape to the region where Francis and his comrades were stationed. The Ghanaians helped alleviate the civilians' hardships, but they were risking their lives in the process. Indeed, in October, Francis and his colleagues came under fire from paramilitary forces, and similar incidents occurred throughout the autumn. At the end of the six months, Francis was simply glad that he'd made it out alive, though at the same time, he felt a profound debt to the soldiers who'd lost their lives in their attempt to restore peace in Lebanon.

* * *

Upon returning home in late 1981, aged 23, Francis was appointed as a secretary to the Discipline Committee involved in the screening of those who'd been accused of corruption and other malpractices. Meanwhile, he also oversaw a group of soldiers loyal to Flight Lieutenant Rawlings; this turned out to be a case of being in the right place at the right time since the latter staged another coup on New Year's Eve of that same year.

Believing that the Limann regime was a so-called 'pack of criminals leading the nation down to total economic ruin', Rawlings led a second coup on 31 December 1981, and this time, he took over permanent leadership of Ghana, presiding over the Provisional National Defence Council (PNDC), a military junta he established as the official government. Initially, older Ghanaians doubted that Rawlings and his colleagues could provide a more effective and less self-interested government than the old politicians. Meanwhile, many young soldiers thought that they could themselves engineer coups to gain power.

However, Rawlings would easily snuff out any attempts to stage an uprising. He promised a return to democracy. However, it was dictatorship that coerced civilians into supporting him. Under Rawlings, there was no freedom of speech, and rather than reforming the army as he supposedly intended, he sank it and gave power to a few select members of Ghana's Ewe tribe.

Francis had supported Rawlings' group completely and had even been prepared to fight for it. So, although he hadn't been called upon to do so, his loyalty was recognised and he was appointed Coordinator of the Revolutionary Committee in the Brong-Ahafo region. In that capacity, he addressed meetings to inform the public about the new government's policies, which, to begin with, had communist leanings. Introducing workers' councils to oversee Ghana's factories, Rawlings even turned to the Soviet Union for support. It soon became apparent that people largely and genuinely appreciated his efforts to transform their country's political and economic status.

Yet although the PNDC claimed to be representative of the people, it lacked experience in creating economic policies leaving Rawlings, like many of his predecessors, to blame economic and social problems on 'trade malpractices and other antisocial activities' carried out by rogue businesspeople. To solve these issues, the junta devised a four-year plan, which included price controls on food. However, while these benefitted the urban population, rural farmers whose income depended on the price of agricultural products were penalised. Just two years into the PNDC's communist experiment, it became clear that this wasn't a viable route, so Rawlings abandoned it and decided to embrace the free market. Ultimately, by the early 1990s, those measures would ensure that Ghana had one of the highest growth rates in Africa. Meanwhile, Rawlings announced presidential elections in 1992, which he won, before being elected a second time four years later and becoming the longest-serving leader in Ghana's history by the time he stepped down in 2001.

* * *

Not long after Rawlings' takeover, and amid the ongoing economic crisis, Francis met Agnes Peprah at the Transport Yard in Accra in 1982. He was travelling with his army friends when he saw her standing by the roadside. For a man who was strictly goal-oriented and didn't care much for distractions, he was shocked to find himself giving her a second glance. In fact, he stared at her for so long, his friends started laughing and teasing him. They knew that he didn't have a girlfriend. So, although he claimed not to be interested, they eagerly urged him to make a move.

Practically shoved towards the girl, Francis decided to talk to her. Beautiful and tall, she made him nervous, and he had never felt nervous around a girl. He ran his hand through his close-cropped hair and licked his lips. However, as he approached her, he sensed from her demeanour that she was scared of him.

This didn't surprise him as soldiers nearly always elicited that reaction, especially from women. Rumour had it that soldiers were dangerous, merciless killers and rapists with only a sense of duty and responsibility to their nation. Those rumours were so rampant that Francis almost started believing them himself. Yet still he approached the girl, and with a warm smile plastered on his face, he was able to get her shoulders to relax. She was wearing a light blue dress that floated around her ankles. Her long, dark hair was swept over her shoulders, and for a moment, as Francis studied her, his hands itched to run his fingers through the shiny strands.

"Why is a beautiful lady like you standing here all on her own?" he asked.

In return, she smiled a little and looked at him with dark, shy eyes that seemed to see into his very soul. With her full lips barely moving, she quietly replied.

"I'm not on my own. I'm here with my older brother. He's just gone to buy our bus tickets so we can travel back to our village."

"What's your name?" Francis asked.

"Agnes."

"And what's the name of your village?"

"Tanoso," she said. "It's near Sunyani."

Hearing this, he left abruptly and rejoined his friends. They teased him mercilessly but he just dragged them off towards the ticket office. Francis couldn't believe what he was doing; he felt like he was suspended in air and watching himself go through the motions. A few minutes later, he returned to Agnes with two tickets and handed them to her. Surprised, she thanked him profusely with a bright smile. His heart skipped a bit. Nodding to acknowledge her gratitude, he clasped his hands together.

"Enjoy your journey. One day, you'll be my wife."

Unsurprisingly, his friends laughed at him for the rest of the day. Francis was not bothered, just anxious about when he would see Agnes again. He wasn't sure when he'd have to leave on another mission, and he was eager to make her his wife before he had to depart once more. So, a few days later, armed with her name and that of her village, he and a few of his army friends travelled to her home so he could ask for her hand in marriage.

However, as soon as they arrived in Tanoso, it was pandemonium. People started running away at the sight of them. Still very young, this amused Francis and his friends so much that they decided to play into it. The moment they arrived at Agnes'ss house, a young woman sitting at the front started panicking and shouting for her mother. When the latter eventually came, she immediately went down on her knees and begged Francis and his friends not to harm them. After Francis urged the older woman to get up again, he explained the reason for his visit, and in response, the woman shared a look with her daughter and they both laughed in relief.

"I'm Mary Boateng," Agnes's mother introduced herself as she ushered them inside.

She called for her older son, who had become the head of the family since the death of Mary's husband, Kwabena Peprah. But although they welcomed Francis and his friends into their home, Agnes's family were hesitant to give the girl away to a soldier. Mary didn't trust the army and proceeded to voice all her misgivings about them, including, but not limited to, how they killed without thinking twice. Not mincing her words, she referred to them as 'monsters'.

Francis understood her attitude and knew that most of her objections were justified. However, he couldn't give up on Agnes, nor could he quit his career. Being in the army defined a lot of his identity as a man. It was his life, and on top of that, he'd left another one behind to build it. Regardless of the guns he wielded and the authority that came with being allowed to kill on behalf of the government, he knew that he wasn't a monster. He loved Agnes, and monsters didn't love. All this and more he told her family, and reluctantly, they finally approved their courtship.

* * *

The upcoming nuptials meant that Francis had to reconnect with his family. Sadly, just a few weeks later, when it was time for his parents to meet Agnes and her relatives, Yaw fell seriously ill. So, it was only Afia and some other family members, including a few of Francis's older siblings, who travelled to Tanoso with him. On the day of the family introductions, a date for the wedding was decided. A marriage list was presented to Francis, which included the bride price, a new suitcase with pieces of African print, jewellery, a copy of the Bible, rings and money for the bride's mother. Agnes'ss older brothers weren't left out either - they would receive *akonta sekan*, which translates as money to thank them for protecting their sister. By Ghanaian standards, it was a relatively short and inexpensive list, but Francis didn't care; he'd have happily handled a more daunting list. The army paid handsomely, and he'd saved up most of the money he'd made since joining up. With his earnings, Francis and Agnes single-handedly planned the ceremony, which was planned to take place in her family home.

When he arrived there on that fateful day, he was welcomed by music from a traditional Adowa group. The female lead singer and backing vocalists accompanied their singing with clapping of hands and ringing a *dawure* (double bell) or an *atoke* (single bell) as well as with percussion instruments. The atmosphere was filled with good cheer and joy, and Francis saw his family seated comfortably in the area reserved for them, looking every inch like the Oppongs that he remembered from his childhood - beautifully attired and bearing all the items on the marriage list.

After his family was officially welcomed, the dowry and the gifts were presented. Francis's brother, George Arthur, the eldest of the Oppong brood, acted as his spokesperson, while Agnes was also represented by her oldest brother. Then Francis was introduced to all present. As he smiled at the crowd, he could feel, for the first time in his life, his face heat up. Then Agnes was invited in. Amid music and dancing, she entered with an entourage of her female friends, all beautifully clad in rich *kente* (traditional Ghanaian cloth made from strips of woven fabric) and adorned with beads. Agnes was literally paraded for all to see and admire her beauty. As Francis stared longingly at his beautiful wife-to-be, his heart threatened to jump out of his chest in excitement. He grew nervous, his palms sweaty, but he remained as calm and still as a rod; it was what was expected of him as a man and especially as a man of the army.

While Agnes walked around the small gathering to shake hands with his family members as a sign of welcoming them, she was showered with compliments.

"Our lovely lady."

"Our well-groomed woman."

Lots of other tributes to her beauty flew from the lips of Francis's mother and his siblings, as well as a few of his army friends who'd been invited to the wedding.

After the introduction, Agnes was asked by her oldest brother if the gifts brought should be accepted, and she responded with a firm, "Yes!" However, he repeated his question three more times before he was finally satisfied enough to take her word for it. She was then presented to the *abusuapanyin* (the head of the family in West Africa's Akan culture) of Francis's family and asked that she be kept as good-looking as she was that day. Finally, she moved towards Francis and sat beside him.

Taking her hand, he interlaced their fingers and smiled at her. She looked so beautiful and regal that he couldn't take his eyes off her. While pieces of advice for the young couple flew from every corner, all he could think about was taking Agnes home and making her his wife in the real sense of the word.

After the ceremony, food was served. There was a banquet of jollof rice, *waakye*, *banku*, okra soup, *kenkey* and fish. Meanwhile, Francis and his new wife went round to greet their guests, thanking them for being part of their big day. His army friends who'd been there when he'd first met Agnes reminded him of his statement that day, and they all burst into laughter.

The day of their wedding marked the start of Francis's and Agnes'ss new life together and the start of a long adventure. The couple went on to live at the army barracks based in Sunyani, in designated family accommodation where they basked in the joy and excitement of life as newlyweds. Part of that excitement was in trying for a baby. However, by the time they'd fully settled into married life, around three months after the wedding, Francis was back on army duty, leaving Agnes at the barracks, and still not pregnant. Over the following months, they continued trying whenever Francis came home on leave with no results. Meanwhile, back in Francis's hometown, Yaw's health was steadily declining and had taken to his deathbed.

* * *

He knew that his time had come, so he asked one of his sons, Kakra, to bring Francis and Agnes to him, so that he could speak to his youngest child one last time. After scrambling to find him, his brother eventually located Francis, who was rushed back home from his duties to have a final conversation with his father.

Francis was devastated about the fact that this was it. He told his father about Agnes'ss fertility issues and Yaw gave her some herbs to help with conceiving. Nevertheless, he was over the moon about their marriage and blessed it, wishing them all the best. He could see that Agnes was perfect for his son.

"You're destined for greatness," he told Francis. "Nothing and no one will be able to harm you."

Those were Yaw's parting words to his last-born, and he passed away not long afterwards, leaving the family to grieve his loss.

4

After Yaw's death, Francis fought internally with himself. At first, he couldn't believe that his father was gone. Sadly, he had to miss the small burial ceremony according to Muslim rites because he had to attend to urgent duties even though his bereavement leave should have started straight away. Not being there to say goodbye made the loss feel even more unreal. Surely, a man who'd pulled ailing people back from the brink of death time and time again couldn't be dead. A depression like he'd never known before started gnawing at Francis, biting his very soul. When he was able to start his two weeks of bereavement leave, he was able to return to the family home. Every day, he expected Yaw to walk through the rickety front door at any moment with an armful of herbs and growling about how many customers he had to care for. At night he stayed awake while the past crept up on him; and to make things worse, for the first few days, Afia locked herself away in her room, refusing to receive any of the many visitors who came to share in her grief. Even her children were completely ignored. Francis wanted to see his mother badly, knowing it would lessen the pain he felt, but she refused him.

Francis was left to attend to the many mourners that included extended family and friends who kept commenting that he had his dad's face and the shape of his head, as well as anything else they could think of. These remarks came from a good place as they were made in a bid to comfort him. Instead, they ended up having the exact opposite effect because hearing all that made Francis miss Yaw even more, which, in turn, made him angry because he'd never get to see his father again.

To add to his misery, Francis felt left out and neglected by his siblings, who he could hear mumbling amongst themselves when they thought he was out of earshot.

"He's a soldier. He sees death almost every day, so he doesn't feel a thing. He probably won't miss him."

In truth, Francis had thought so too. He'd been convinced that the military had toughened him up so well that he would remain unaffected by his father's death. As it turned out, coupled with the snobbish glances and comments from his siblings, he was the one who felt most hurt out of all of them. In fact, he felt like an outcast in his own home, and after the first few days he wanted to leave. He longed to be on a mission, in the Sambisa, anywhere, shooting down enemy troops or doing just about anything rather than being with his family. Francis had never felt so lonely in his entire life. The days stretched so bleakly, he thought he'd die from it. In his darkest moments, he wanted life to end with Yaw's death since he couldn't believe that life could go on as if nothing had changed.

Soon, Francis became filled to the brim with anger, at death and life in general. Bitterness ate him up. He couldn't fully grasp why his father had died. One moment he had seen him ill, and the next he was gone. He felt cheated by life. Yes, Yaw had been fairly old, but Francis was the youngest in the family and therefore hadn't had the time to fully enjoy him, not to mention the fact that being in the army didn't allow him much freedom to see his family.

This was the first death of a close relative that Francis had experienced, and the pain was far beyond what he'd imagined it would be. The man who meant so much to him was gone forever and he partly blamed himself for Yaw's death — not being there to administer care when his father had been on his dying bed. Francis should've been the one to make his medicine. He could feel that his siblings blamed him too because his decision to join the army had taken a toll on their dad, which had slowly led to his death. Francis believed his father had never forgiven him for abandoning the herbal business against his wishes and stubbornly joining the army instead. With no one to continue his lifelong trade, Yaw had now taken his pain to the grave. Regretting that he had been so hard-headed, Francis thought about taking to drink to dull the ache; he knew that if he did, things would not end well because if he became addicted to alcohol, which could have easily happened, he would be thrown out of the military.

* * *

After having been back at the barracks for several weeks, Francis was finally and painfully able to accept the death of his father and come to terms with its significance. Meanwhile, Ghana's financial crisis hadn't abated — in fact, it had exploded and was now too much for the government to handle. So, suddenly, Francis was facing the prospect of the army getting drawn into the country's economic turmoil. Jerry Rawlings again tried to address the issues by implementing Soviet-style policies like price controls on food and rent. He also reinstated many employees who had been dismissed by the previous administration and declared a freeze on further layoffs. But his solutions to Ghana's persistent economic problems were akin to pouring water into a palm basket.

Rawlings' alignment with the Eastern bloc was based on the expectation that those countries would provide immediate and continuous support to Ghana. However, his supposed allies failed to do so because they had enough problems of their own and weren't able to help. As a result, Ghana faced economic ruin because the disastrous socialist policies that Rawlings had implemented severely reduced incentives for production and therefore investment (both domestic and foreign), leading to a decline in savings among the population. Consequently, the economy didn't recover as quickly as Rawlings had envisioned, and throughout 1982, his popularity as well as that of the PNDC government plummeted. Both its leader and other members now constantly found themselves on the defensive, trying to prevent coups and unrest. In that process, opposition leaders were jailed, and at least one person who'd been convicted of plotting a coup was executed.

Although their reforms were unpopular and failing, Rawlings and his Secretary of Finance remained determined to nurture national development and improve people's livelihoods. However, the scale of the challenges they faced grew even bigger in early 1983, when over a million Ghanaians who'd left for greener pastures in Nigeria were expelled, further reducing the prospects of employment in their home country.

At the time, Francis had a best friend who he thought of as an older brother since he was about ten years his senior, a Robert Amofa. He'd met Robert in the army in Sunyani, not far from Agnes's village. Robert was already friends with another soldier, Boat, when Francis met both of them as a new recruit. The three of them were very similar in personality and had shared interests, so they became firm friends. At one point, they were nicknamed 'The Three Musketeers'. Whenever they wanted to smoke weed or meet up somewhere without anyone else knowing about it, they called each other 'Saman', like a secret whistle.

However, in 1980, before Rawlings had taken power from Hilla Limann, Robert had left for the UK, so it was just Francis and Boat living through Ghana's current troubles. Boat complained bitterly about the decline of the economy, saying that he'd never be able to take care of his two sons in these circumstances. They laughed it off, but Francis knew that Boat was making a good point and one that he knew well. Whilst Agnes was still hoping to have a child, she looked after Asantewaa, the young daughter of one of her older sisters, Adwoa, who'd also left for the UK in search of a better life. Francis and Agnes had taken the little girl in with them as a toddler and raised her at the 3rd Battalion Infantry Liberation Barracks in Sunyani. Agnes devoted her entire time to taking care of and becoming a mother figure to Asantewaa. In the midst of Ghana's ongoing crisis, they were like a little family. Francis showered the girl with gifts and played with her on the rare occasions when he was back home. From that vantage point, Francis could understand Boat's concerns, even as he questioned his friend about what it was like to be a dad.

"You better find out for yourself," Boat chuckled.

Yet to Francis, the catastrophe that Ghana had become didn't seem like a good place to have, let alone raise, a child. He didn't know any more whether he should be sad or relieved that his wife was yet to give birth; he was so confused. When two of Agnes's sisters in the UK started talking about inviting them over so they could finally meet him, having missed the wedding, Francis felt this invitation presented an opportunity that came at the most perfect time. Everyone knew that 'a visit' could quickly become something more permanent, a new dawn in a different country when there seemed to be no way forward at home.

Yet he was torn, not being the kind of person who ran away from his problems. Plus, he was apprehensive about leaving the army since he didn't know what else he could be but a soldier. He shared his fears with Boat, who slapped a hand across his shoulder, eyes wide as he muttered his congratulations.

"You're so lucky, you know that? You're going to be out of here and out of this dump," he said, gesturing around the makeshift army canteen where they were sitting. "Say hi to Robert when you get there. And don't you dare miss me!" he joked.

Francis pulled Boat into a tight hug. "I will miss you," he said.

In view of how excited his friend was for him, Francis couldn't believe that he'd been afraid to venture out of his comfort zone simply because he didn't know what other jobs he could do. Judging by Boat's reaction, simply being in the UK was much more important than his fears of losing his career. Nevertheless, when he saw Agnes again during one of his brief visits home, he still wasn't sure.

"What would I do when we get to the UK?"

"My sisters will look into it," she assured him. "Nobody would expect you sit around doing nothing. In fact, I may even get one myself," she said, giggling softly.

Francis shook his head. "I don't know, Aggie. Being a soldier is all I've ever known. It's all I'm trained to be. What if I can't be anything else?"

Putting a hand on his shoulders, Agnes looked deep into his eyes. "You weren't born a soldier Kojo. You grew to love it. And I'm sure you'll grow to love the UK and the jobs that will come our way there. My sisters will take care of this, trust me. And Asantewaa will get to see her mum."

This convinced Francis, and they both started talking about how they'd thrive in the UK. Agnes was very excited about the prospect of getting a job. She wanted four children, two boys and two girls. Although Francis would have wanted more, the thought of the bad economy stopped him from starting an argument. In any case, he was so busy in the army that he didn't have much time to think about their future plans. Having initially supported the Rawlings government, he was now beginning to hate it since it had become a total disaster. Hope for the nation was ebbing away steadily, and being in the thick of things, Francis and his colleagues understood that it would take a long time for the situation to return to normal — if indeed it ever would, and without any drastic action.

In theory, Francis earned enough to take care of Agnes and Asantewaa. Things were so bad though that even if you had the money, you couldn't get what you wanted. The economic situation was compounded by severe drought and bushfires, which destroyed about one third of Ghana's cocoa farms. This brought severe food shortages and famine in various parts of the country. Ghanaians had to queue for basic essentials such as bread, sugar and maize. In their struggle to survive, many of them were forced to practically become beggars in their own home.

It was a sore sight to behold, and one that Francis and his colleagues were constantly in the midst of as they tried to control the teeming crowds of hungry, angry people. In addition, due to the drought, Ghana's hydroelectric power plant at Adwoaombo Dam ran out of water, creating power shortages across the country that led to low productivity in various manufacturing industries.

Francis' family wasn't having it easy either. Some of his siblings had lost their jobs and were essentially living hand to mouth. Francis tried to help, but there was a limit to what he could spare. Soon, a few of his siblings that he couldn't immediately assist began to backbite and make an enemy of him.

Meanwhile, Afia was more worried about Francis being in the army amid the countrywide chaos, fearing that she'd lose him too, just like she'd lost Yaw. She voiced her worries and often begged him to quit and return home. However, Francis knew that if he left the army without a good reason, he wouldn't be able to provide for his family in any way. So, it was the army or nothing.

Finally, under pressure from the Ghanaian people and with no financial help forthcoming from the Eastern bloc, Rawlings and the PNDC government executed a spectacular U-turn to restore economic stability. Despite their previous socialist/Marxist posturing and their attacks on Western capitalist ideology, to them, the best alternative to addressing the issues at hand appeared to be to reconsider Ghana's relationship with the West and ask for assistance from the International Monetary Fund (IMF) and the World Bank. However, the members of the PNDC were divided on this decision. One group argued that the proposed realignment contradicted the government's founding principles. Meanwhile, a second group composed of pragmatists and economic reformers supported Rawlings's about-turn as they believed that this was the only solution to the economic crisis that was consuming the country.

As if things couldn't get worse, Agnes became extremely ill. So, Francis was tossed back and forth, dividing his attention between being a soldier and a husband. Oftentimes, Agnes felt so unwell that he feared he was going to lose her, but every time, she'd come back from the brink of death. Francis suggested that Agnes go and stay with family while she was recovering, so she and Asantewaa travelled back to her village to be with her mother for a while. Agnes voiced her worries for him, insisting that he should leave the disintegrating government. All this made Francis think that she'd fallen ill because of loneliness, so he promised her to be home more often. However, as they would discover soon enough, Agnes'ss ailment hadn't been caused by loneliness.

* * *

By mid-1983, Ghana was not only close to bankruptcy but also receiving criticism from human rights groups as Ghanaian citizens outside the country brought the PNDC's tactics and the plight of political prisoners to the attention of Amnesty International. Meanwhile, Ghana's various Defence Committees were plagued by internal strife as Rawlings and his government had no formal operating guidelines. Neither did they offer any direct financial assistance, which meant that the Defence Committees were responsible for their own planning and operations. This ill-defined set-up sometimes resulted in conflicts between different committees as well as within the PNDC. Although the government's lack of administrative and financial support meant that crucial public work issues went unaddressed, fines were imposed on community members who were deemed 'not enthusiastic enough' about the PNDC's policies. These fines extracted from so-called 'corrupt counter-revolutionary segments of society' were supposed to help fund the Defence Committees' activities. Yet instead, they became another example of mismanagement.

On 23 March 1984, military dissidents based in two neighbouring countries, Côte d'Ivoire in the west and Togo in the east, invaded Ghana to overthrow the government. The leader of the Cote d'Ivoire group and his men were arrested, while the Togolese group was discovered in the Ningo area in southern Ghana where they were apprehended by the local Defence Committees.

After a brief interrogation at the Air Force station, they were executed one after the other by a firing squad.

The PNDC responded strongly to public acts of dissent by framing its critics as counter-revolutionaries and arresting them, with sentencing carried out in a hastily created tribunal system that operated outside the existing legal structures. Such repression was apparently justified to uphold the government's integrity and its need to punish 'crimes against the people'. The state even used physical force to clamp down on relatively minor transgressions. For instance, if members of the Defence Committees were caught trying to resell food they'd been able to buy at reduced prices, they would be subject to imprisonment and torture by the same security forces that employed them.

Things became unbearable. Francis received many letters from Afia urging him to return home as she worried that he might get caught up in a tense situation and lose his life. In an attempt to alleviate her concerns, he visited her more frequently. But this did not assuage her fears and she would cry bitterly each time he left.

By the end of 1984, the Defence Committees, which all played a significant role in perpetuating state violence, were coming under increasing criticism for corruption. A week before a November meeting with aid donors involving the World Bank, they were dissolved into the Committees for the Defence of the Revolution (CDR) — presumably so Rawlings could keep the World Bank happy and retain its support as the Defence Committees were, by now, viewed as divisive and disruptive. CDRs were to organise communal labour for community development projects under the leadership of traditional authorities, including chiefs, whose input had been excluded when the Defence Committees had been in charge. However, this new set-up left urban workers and students increasingly frustrated as they were unable to influence policies or even just express public criticism of Rawlings and other decision-makers.

Not only were protests about the regime's excesses and the lack of democracy banned, the media was also expected to project a perfect image of the government by defending its initiatives. To that end, the PNDC even hired and dismissed editorial staff of state-owned publications, while the Newspaper Licensing Law that was reintroduced in 1983 discouraged the establishment and freedom of private media. The result was a culture of silence where no one dared to complain when soldiers forced market traders to sell goods at 'affordable' prices. All this left Francis and many other Ghanaians baffled by Rawlings' so-called revolution, as well as revolted by his regime's strong-arm tactics. However, with discontent brewing, the PNDC realised it needed to demonstrate that it was actively considering steps towards constitutionalism and civilian rule. To move in the desired direction, 'Rawlings & Co' had to weaken the influence and credibility of all antagonistic groups while creating the necessary political structures that would bring more and more Ghanaians into the process of national reconstruction.

To this end, the PNDC proposed the establishment of district assemblies, and to further signal its determination to bring about a new political dawn for Ghana, the National Commission for Democracy (NCD) was officially launched in January 1985. A couple of months later, on 28 March, Francis was appointed the CDR Coordinator in view of the massive role he'd played in the PNDC. However, after all the upheaval across the country, he was far from invested in the government by now and was only part of it because he knew he couldn't back out.

On the morning that his appointment was announced, Francis trembled in his heavy boots. Amid clapping and several congratulatory slaps on the back from colleagues, friends and foes, he shakily walked towards his superior's office. It was the first time he'd been honoured to grace the place. However, while his shoulders were held high, he couldn't get his hands to stop shaking enough to render a proper salute. His superior didn't seem to mind, though, as he smiled smugly at him.

"Not many are lucky enough to get this position, Sergeant Oppong. I hope you don't make me regret it."

Sitting in his large mahogany chair, this ruthless man maintained his smile and unwavering stare. Francis managed a nod and a short acknowledgement as his ears continued to ring. Absent-mindedly, he read the multiple documents he had to sign, and then he was handed a little silver plaque engraved with his new title.

After leaving the office, Francis was halfway down a long, narrow corridor when he decided to go back and ask his superior why the previous coordinator had been removed. However, he changed his mind almost instantly because he didn't want the superior to think of him as scared or weak, since that would only have led to a campaign of intimidation.

Boat teased Francis about his new position and insisted that as the new CDR Coordinator, perhaps he could make some changes to the inadequate government. Yet Francis knew as well as anyone that this was just wishful thinking. There was nothing he could do. In fact, as the CDR Coordinator, he was just a pawn in the hands of those higher up. He would be told what to do and how to do it, taking him back to his army training days. Only this was worse because here, he knew what he ought to do, but he wasn't allowed to do it as the Rawlings government was like a staircase to the heavens that could never be reached.

That said, as the coordinator of such a special and important committee, he was allowed a lot of freedom, as long as it didn't interfere with the affairs of the government. Nevertheless, Francis found himself pining to go home, even though he wasn't sure how they would feel about his appointment. The truth was, he was scared for his wife, his mother and siblings, especially if something bad were to happen to him because of his new position. They would never forgive him.

He'd thought that being in the army would give him so much power, power to do and undo, but that wasn't the case. What little power he had was, in fact, directed by the people above him, which, conversely, made him feel powerless, and on top of that, useless. He'd dreamt of a better Ghana from the moment he'd entered his first training ground, but he could have done without those dreams because his country was slowly being deprived of its very essence. It was a chaotic mess, with Rawlings redesigning committees just to escape the wrath of human rights groups, while his policies remained in place and continued to fail.

A few nights after his appointment, Francis, Boat and a few of their colleagues went for drinks to 'celebrate' his appointment. Francis only took the opportunity to drown his worries in alcohol, even if it was just for a few hours. He was fully aware that he was given the position because those in charge thought that he could be manipulated and controlled. He also knew that it was true because essentially his entire life, he'd only ever taken orders. His compliance and reliability, which were great qualities to have at other times, were his undoing now. Yet as he reminisced about the past, Francis decided that perhaps his friend was right and he really could make some changes to the way things were done. So, there and then, he made up his mind to do whatever he had to do in order to make change happen.

5

Francis's new office was small, nothing like he'd expected. It was just one of the abandoned storerooms on the far end of the barracks, tight and airless. All morning, as Francis sat behind his equally small desk, he felt suffocated. It was only when CDR members and civilians came to seek his input that he began to feel better. He wiped his sweaty palms on his dark khaki trousers and sent for Boat. When his friend arrived, Francis shared the decision he'd made on their night out. Boat just looked at him like he'd lost his mind.

"I was only teasing when I said you should make changes," he admitted anxiously.

Francis wasn't surprised by his alarm because he, too, felt lost. "I know," he said, "but it doesn't matter. My mind is made up."

There were a few CDR members he could dare to trust not to rat him out. So, with the help of Boat, he sent them shorthand notes outlining his plans. Soon, they arrived at his tiny office for a private meeting, where Francis explained how dissatisfied he was with those

CDR members he deemed 'lawful troublemakers'. His intention was to bring an end to their behaviour, or at the very least, to tame them.

Five of the soldiers present agreed with his plans, but not one of them was willing to do anything about it. They were all scared; after all, they had families to consider and given how harsh the government's policies tended to be, they doubted that the PNDC would compensate the relatives of soldiers who'd lost their lives in a rebellion against it. Francis couldn't blame them for their attitude, so he let them go.

Boat, on the other hand, praised Francis's bravery, and although he wasn't eager either, he was willing to support him. So, from then on, the two of them would occasionally stroll to the local markets and assist women who'd lost their wares and goods to corrupt CDR members. They would hand them some money, and if any older women needed their shops to be rebuilt, they even paid for labourers to construct better buildings. In the grand scheme of things, these were just little gestures that meant little in the context of the chaos consuming the whole country. Still, with these acts, Francis felt a sense of fulfilment.

While he'd envisioned helping the masses when he'd fantasised about wielding power at the tender age of 15, he was happy to now be in a place where he could make positive changes, no matter how little. In a way, it felt like being back in his father's house and administering herbal concoctions to the sick. Although he knew that the troubles in Ghana weren't going to go away with a single drop of his concoction, Francis was pleased that he was doing something meaningful instead of being holed up in a suffocating office while slowly losing his mind. However, the risk of what he was doing was high. Twice, they were caught handing money to women, and they were rigorously interrogated. Fortunately, the authority he held as the CDR Coordinator meant that his excuses couldn't be questioned.

Twice, Boat threatened to give up, and eventually, even Francis had to come to terms with the fact that it was too risky to fight a lonely battle. If his superiors got wind of what he did in the market and elsewhere, not only would he lose his new position, but he could also get arrested, which was one of the worst fears of every soldier.

Meanwhile, the recent Western-supported Economic Recovery Program (ERP) had injected hundreds of millions of dollars into Ghana's economy. Yet the best that could be said was that there'd been a marginal improvement in the economic picture since Rawlings had abandoned his links to the Soviet Bloc. The hopes of a depressed nation had been raised, but by mid-1985, a few months after Francis's appointment, Rawlings admitted that his revolution hadn't created the 'new democracy' that he'd intended. What was this new democracy supposed to be exactly? Well, it was where the population participated fully in the government's decisions while benefitting from enhanced equality, economic opportunity and a redistribution of wealth, as he and his allies had promised.

However, Rawlings' admission to his failures did nothing to change the fates of millions of Ghanaians. In fact, it was safe to say that there was no ray of hope, and by the end of the year, Francis and some of his colleagues had become so dissatisfied with the dictatorship-style government that they sent a letter to high-ranking officials to express their view that democracy should be restored.

Francis had graciously handled the writing of the letter, and with great pride in his heart, he had sent it off on 3 December 1985. It might have taken longer than he had anticipated, but he was excited to have successfully pulled off his initial plan. However, his excitement was short-lived.

That very evening, after he'd made plans to visit Agnes and tell her about the unfolding development, Francis and about ten of his colleagues were rounded up and arrested. Amid brief struggles, with rifles being stuck into their ribs, they were pushed into a waiting and filthy truck. Given his position as the leader of the arrested soldiers, Francis, although handcuffed, bravely questioned the casually dressed men.

"Who are you, and where are you taking us?"

He was answered by a huge man with a face that could induce nightmares. Francis assumed that this was the leader of the gang.

"You only speak when you're spoken to!" bellowed the man.

Although Francis wasn't scared of him, he couldn't risk riling the man and thereby starting a fight as the people who were arresting him and his allies were armed to the teeth. Much to Francis's surprise, they were taken to the headquarters of the Special Investigation Branch (SIB), which was responsible for investigating criminal offences committed by military personnel. Francis hadn't committed any crime worthy of the SIB's attention, so he knew this had to be about the letter he'd sent earlier that day.

Pushed out of the trucks, he and his allies stumbled to find their footing amid the men barking and issuing mindless orders in their faces. Then they were taken to the guardroom to be formally arrested by the regimental police, the SIB men. There were three of them, and none wore a uniform, so they could have passed for civilians. The shabby guardroom was fairly large but had only a tiny window close to the high ceiling. There were no chairs and the SIB men made Francis and the rest of the soldiers sit on the cold stone floor.

"I want to see my superior!" Francis protested.

"You can't," came the reply. "Because you've all been arrested for a conspiracy to overthrow the lawful government of Ghana."

Hearing this, Francis limply sat down on the floor next to his colleagues. He knew someone had betrayed them. As the three SIB men barked questions and hovered around them like chickens in a cornfield, Francis had never felt so humiliated in his entire life. He couldn't understand how he could hold such a lofty position in the army only to be reduced to nothing in the blink of an eye.

"It was just a letter," Francis' mumbled under his breath.

Unfortunately, the shortest of the three SIB men heard him, and turning sharply, he slapped him across the mouth. Then he dragged him up by the collar and hissed at him.

"You! What are you whispering about?"

The two held a tense staring match that lasted almost a minute before Francis was roughly shoved to the floor. There was a snap that made him wince in pain, and Francis was sure that he'd broken a bone.

"Who amongst you came up with the plan to overthrow the government?" another SIB man bellowed.

Francis sucked his lips in and remained quiet. He knew how this would pan out. As a matter of fact, he knew very well because back when he'd allowed himself to be a government pawn, he'd been part of the Discipline Committee that punished stubborn civilians and wayward soldiers.

Faced with silence, the SIB men became angrier and angrier. Legs pacing the length and breadth of the room, they lashed snake-like whips on the soldiers' bodies, eliciting loud screams from them. When gun bayonets were eventually brought into the room, Francis's men started to yap, blaming him for leading them to their deaths. So, with those weapons, the SIB men finally got all the answers they wanted, with every finger pointed at Francis.

As the short SIB man approached him, a gun bayonet dangling from his hand, Francis's mind drifted to Agnes, young and beautiful, and at home waiting for his return. His heart twisted in pain at his impending death. He was yet to fully enjoy his marriage. With a demanding career as a soldier, he cherished every brief moment he shared with his wife, and he wanted more. He wanted to grow old with her, have lots of children and fill their home with warm love. As the seconds slowly ticked by though, Francis knew that he had failed in his promises to protect and never leave her.

He knew she was still talking to her sisters in the UK about the plans for their trip there, and he wondered what would happen if he was never found again. At that moment, all he wanted was to get a message to her and tell her about his predicament since he knew that it was only a matter of time before she'd become sick with worry. Being married to a soldier wasn't easy, and he loved her even more for her strength and resilience in keeping the home front strong without him. Though on the flipside, this was also the reason why he now felt so guilty about putting himself out in the open without considering the potential dire consequences, which might include losing Agnes forever.

After being subjected to torture several times during the course of that terrible evening, a breathless Francis finally fell into a restless sleep. Then, just a few hours later, he was rudely awakened by a splash of cold water on his body. Drenched and shivering from the cold, he gaped helplessly at his colleagues as the SIB men started another round of interrogation.

"Who and where are the rest of your accomplices?" they hissed, the question being directed at Francis.

However, he could only stammer, his teeth clattering from the cold seeping into his body. A hard slap across his cheek caused the blood to return to his face as he muttered the only truth he knew: "There's no one else."

Yet the men didn't believe him. Instead, they cackled amongst themselves, and one of them, in a fit of rage, attacked Francis with a gun bayonet, slicing through his left hand. Sucking back a scream from the shattering pain, Francis slapped his good hand across his injured one to stop the flow of blood. His eyes rolled behind their sockets as he fell and hit his head hard on the stone floor. Barely conscious, his mind reeled with thoughts of Agnes as numbness swept over him.

Seeing that he was injured, the SIB men roughly grabbed him and hauled him out of the guardroom, taking him outside the building, where they instructed some of their colleagues to drive him to the 3rd Battalion Military Hospital known as the 3rd Military Reception Service (3MRS) for treatment.

* * *

About three weeks later, as Christmas arrived without Francis being in touch, Agnes became extremely worried because it was unlike him to have been uncontactable for such a long spell. She could feel it in her gut that something was terribly wrong. After sharing her fears with her family, they were able to get hold of an inside man who told them Francis had been arrested by the SIB and was currently in 3MRS. Agnes begged one of Francis' colleagues to go there with her, and with his help, she was able to visit her husband.

On the day of her visit, she walked gingerly to his bed carrying a large dish filled with home-cooked food. Then, when she saw the state he was in, she collapsed on the rickety bed beside him, weeping. The dish of food had barely survived her fall.

"Stop crying, please," Francis quietly begged her. "Look, I'm lucky to have survived."

While that was true, he could only hope to be able to defend himself sufficiently to escape the long arm of injustice that was the government. There was a strong possibility that he might be arraigned in court, but he hoped it wouldn't come to that.

"The humiliation would be too much to bear," he told his wife. "I would prefer just to get executed."

Agnes shook her head bitterly, rejecting the idea of death and pleading with him once more to leave the army. "Please come back home with me," she whispered, crying, as she held on to Francis's hand.

"I can't, Aggie," he replied. "At least not yet," he quietly added, while watching the guard by the door, who seemed very interested in their conversation.

"I hate this," Agnes cried. "I hate that you're a soldier. Promise me you'll come back to me."

Francis made the promise even though he knew that he wouldn't be able to keep it.

*   *   *

When Agnes told her family what had happened to her husband, their plans to travel to the UK now became urgent. They had to escape as soon as possible. However, after three weeks in 3MRS, Francis was considered to be well enough by the doctor. Just after Christmas, he was sent back to the SIB headquarters.

The guardroom was exactly as he'd last seen it, but he couldn't recognise any of his colleagues any more. They looked worse than he did, even though he'd narrowly escaped the shackles of death. Their eyes protruded from their sockets, and they were so starved that Francis could see their ribs through their flimsy shirts. Those same shirts were now covered in holes, leaving them almost naked. There was a single jug of water on the floor, in the corner of the room, and it seemed like that was all they'd been surviving on. Meanwhile, the room stank to high heaven from their unwashed bodies. As he took in the unacceptable state of degradation of his colleagues, Francis was furious at the SIB men. However, there was absolutely nothing he could do to help his colleagues, some of whom could barely keep their heads steady on their shoulders as they watched him sit down beside them again.

"I'm so sorry," he muttered, for lack of anything else to say. However, they didn't even seem to hear him.

From then on, almost every day, one soldier was taken away each day. One by one, their number dwindled. None of them returned and Francis could only allow himself to imagine their fate.

By the end of December 1985, all of his colleagues had disappeared, leaving only Francis in the guardroom. It was at this point that he dared to accept that the reason for their disappearance was nothing but foul play; either his colleagues had been removed to be executed, or he'd been left behind because it was he who was going to be eliminated. He knew how the military worked. The rules of the game were plain as day, especially as the SIB men continued to sneer at him constantly yet leave him alone. In Francis' mind, they were without a doubt waiting for a set time to snuff him out. When they started to feed him half-decent food, he knew that his hunch was right. Realising that his life was in grave danger, Francis thought long and hard and decided to use his military skills to escape from the guardroom.

On the rare occasion when he was left alone with no guard in sight, he did some push-ups to strengthen his injured hand. However, as the weeks passed, his escape plan no longer appeared feasible since the SIB men continued to regularly check the guardroom. There was always one stationed inside the room. None of them ever talked to him, and he didn't address them either.

On the 3rd March 1986, Francis lucked out. That night, the commander stationed inside the dimly lit guardroom to watch him was drunk and had fallen asleep, complete with loud snoring. Francis knew that his one moment had come. Unable to believe his luck, he quietly stumbled up and checked on the commander's state. Cautiously, he waved a hand across the man's face. The man's eyelashes fluttered slightly, but apart from that, nothing happened. With his heart in his mouth, Francis then slapped a hand on the man's large arm. Again, he didn't react. So, Francis proceeded to check on the security guards at the front door. The lone guard there leaned against the wall, far from the guardroom, seemingly preoccupied with the cigarette between his fingers as smoke billowed above his head.

Francis hesitated as he considered what would happen to him if he got caught. If he didn't get shot on sight, he'd probably never see the light of day again anyway since the army was ruthless and didn't show any mercy. He also knew that if he didn't try to escape, he'd be executed regardless. And for what? Simply because he was fed up, like everyone else, with the injustice and chaos of the government and had decided to speak out.

Springing into action, Francis quickly put on several abandoned stinky jackets that were lying on the floor to mask his scent. He tiptoed out of the guardroom and moved toward the low perimeter wall near the edge of the compound and which was a relic of rough stones topped with rusted barbed wire. Using the 'ghost walk' — a tactical exercise he'd mastered in training to jump high walls — he vaulted the wall. Landing on the other side with a painful scrape on his knees, he winced in pain and steadied himself on the uneven ground outside. Picking himself up from the ground, he dusted his palms on his trousers and ducked along the low shrubs surrounding the building. The cold night air hit his face as he glanced back at the guardroom, now a faint glow behind him, before disappearing into the shadows of the surrounding grounds. Each step was significant as it took him further from his prison and closer to freedom.

He knew that it was only a matter of time before they realised that he had escaped which in turn would trigger a man hunt. His goal was to put enough distance between him and the guards before that happened. For hours, he walked and walked until he finally reached Agnes's village, Tanoso, where he would remain for the next two months.

6

The days grew longer. Agnes felt very lonely. With no communication from Francis since she'd visited him at the hospital a few weeks before, she was anxious and deeply worried about his well-being. If she managed to sleep at night, she'd always wake up in a cold sweat from the nightmares that grew worse and persistent.

One hot afternoon, some angry-looking soldiers barged into Agnes's family home where she'd been staying for the past few months since Francis had disappeared. They wielded ugly guns and brandished them menacingly. When her mother, Mary, saw the soldiers, she immediately collapsed and passed out. Left in fear and shivering, Agnes crouched down to revive her. When Mary eventually came to, the soldiers explained their reason for coming.

"We are looking for Francis Oppong. Where is he?" they demanded.

At the mention of her husband's name, Agnes immediately grabbed a soldier by the leg.

"Where is Francis?" she asked pleadingly.

The soldier glared at her and shook off her hands. "Tell the truth, or you'll suffer the consequences," he snapped.

Agnes whimpered, embarrassed beyond words that she had no idea where her husband was. At the same time, she was even more scared now about what might have happened to him if he was missing, and about what might happen if the soldiers found him. She desperately wanted to find Francis but with the army also searching for him, she wasn't so sure anymore. When the soldiers mentioned that they were heading to Francis' family home, Agnes knew that she had to get there before them. So, after successfully calming Mary down, she pushed Asantewaa into her bosom and found a driver in the village.

Agnes cried all the way to the Ashanti region, and by the time she arrived at the village of Kuntanse Yasi, her eyes were red. From the car, she took a shortcut to the house and, as she'd hoped, arrived before the soldiers had. She immediately alerted Afia about the soldiers. Then, just before she'd even finished telling her about her ordeal, the front door was kicked open. There were shouts and screams from the neighbours. The noise distracted Afia, and she remained confused by Agnes's explanation until she was forcefully dragged outside the house by a soldier.

Their method of interrogation was terrible. They didn't care about Afia's age as they barked at her like dogs, threatening hellfire and brimstone. The only thing Afia could understand amidst her fear was that they wanted to know where Francis was, and they wanted him immediately.

"I've not seen him in months," Afia croaked, her cheeks wet with tears. "I've lost my Yaw, and now you've taken my son too!"

She crumbled to the ground, her shoulders shaking with anger and deep pain. George Arthur, Francis' older brother, who had been visiting, tried to convince the soldiers to stop harassing his mother. He really tried to be reasonable with them, but they remained stubborn; one even punched George square in the jaw. Incensed, he threw caution to the wind and retaliated, pulling one of the soldiers closest to him into a fistfight. However, another punch in his face landed George on the floor. He fell so hard and unexpectedly that he had the wind knocked out of him. Agnes rushed over and helped him up. The soldiers ignored them and split into two groups, half of them barging into the house to search every nook and cranny to make sure that Francis wasn't hiding somewhere; the other half remained outside with Agnes and the rest of the family, closely watching them.

Agnes embraced Afia and said some comforting words, but Francis' heartbroken mother was inconsolable, tears streaming down her flushed cheeks. Meanwhile, George had recovered from his fall and barged into the house. One of the soldiers outside followed him and grabbed his arm roughly and pinned him to the wall.

"Let go of my son!" screeched Afia, but her words fell on deaf ears.

The search inside her home went on for ages. When the soldiers eventually came out of the house, Agnes wondered why they had spent so much time in there considering how small it was. They nodded to a soldier with a huge scar on his face, who seemed to be the team leader.

"You don't want to give him up, do you?" the scar-faced man hissed, his bloodshot eyes boring into George before resting on Afia.

"If I knew where he was, I wouldn't tell the likes of you anyway," George managed to reply from where he remained pinned on the wall.

The soldier holding him up then released him, so that he slumped down the wall to the ground.

"We'll be back," Scar Face promised ominously.

Then he signalled to his men, who all trotted and jumped into their dirty green trucks and drove off, leaving a large plume of dust in their wake.

It was only then that the neighbours who had hidden in their homes at the sight of the soldiers unlocked their front doors and emerged again. They sympathised with Afia and offered comforting words, but she remained numb and refused to speak. Agnes, her heart aching from the dawning realisation that her husband wasn't only missing but must have done something terribly wrong to warrant such harassment, also refused to speak. She held Afia by the waist, and together, they stumbled into the house before shutting the broken front door.

George remained shaken from the soldiers' harassment. When everything had quietened down, he went around the village and looked for Francis' childhood friends — the ones he'd grown up with before leaving for the army. However, none of them seemed to be in Kuntanse Yasi anymore, and just like Francis, had all seemed to have vanished into thin air.

*   *   *

Agnes cried daily, fearing that even if Francis was alive, he'd be executed when the soldiers eventually found him. No matter how he'd tried to make light of his work, she'd always felt trouble looming. Months passed, but there was no news from him or even his colleague who had escorted her to 3MRS to visit Francis. He would have been the one to relay messages if Francis was in need. She knew that things must have got worse, but her hands were tied since she wasn't allowed into the SIB headquarters. She had gone there herself, taking Asantewaa along to appeal to the soldiers' conscience. The heartless men had turned them away without blinking.

Agnes did not give up though. Instead of just going home, she decided to wait near the front gates of the barracks to see if she could find Francis' colleague. Nothing. It seemed that he had gone AWOL too. Had he been silenced? Agnes knew that it was the way of the military and that was one of the many reasons she hated the army. Yes, she had married a soldier, but that had not changed her views whatsoever.

She pondered over the irony. The thing was that Francis had been a smooth talker and very romantic. He'd literally swept her off her feet with his lively charm. Her siblings had warned her and they couldn't understand what she saw in him. Of course, they didn't need to; it was enough that Agnes understood how much she loved her husband-to-be, and she loved him enough to wait for him day and night while he was out and about carrying out his sworn duties to the nation. A crumbling nation. A nation that unjustly detained citizens and even executed them without conscience. A nation that had driven Francis to speak up. Agnes couldn't imagine how she'd survive if Francis never returned. However, she kept her hopes alive. She communicated her fears to her siblings and decided that as soon as she found him, they were going to leave Ghana for the UK. Her sisters there agreed and promised to speed up the process to obtain the required travel documents.

As she stayed with her family for the time being, Agnes surrounded herself with her childhood friends. She had fun, but nothing could fill the void that Francis had left. The hole in her heart grew bigger with every passing day. Then the relative peace was shattered by the soldiers' return.

They trashed the family home ... again ... but this time, breaking chairs and tables and just about pulling the bricks down. As the soldiers were turning the house upside down, Agnes'ss older brother, Charles, walked in. He was an assistant superintendent with the police, an important role within the force, so a very well-respected man. During the first attack, Charles had been away on duty and only heard about the destruction after the fact, but this time he arrived in the middle of the chaos. He stopped in the doorway, stunned by the sight of splintered furniture and soldiers tearing through the rooms. His anger rose as he realised the family's home was being reduced to rubble right before his eyes. As soon as the soldiers recognised him, they stopped their wanton acts of destruction. Clearly, they respected his authority and calmly explained things to him. Swearing on his badge, Charles promised to find Francis and get him back to detention. The soldiers didn't seem to believe him, but they couldn't question his word either, so they left.

7

That walk towards Tanoso, on that March night of 1986 when he had escaped from the SIB headquarters was the hardest Francis had ever made. With the injuries he'd sustained along the way, he was a terrible sight to behold. His trousers were ripped to shreds from thorns and bushes, so he'd pulled off one of the jackets he'd grabbed during his escape, tore it to shreds and used the pieces to stem the bleeding from his legs. He felt extremely weak and looked a shadow of his former self. Anyone who saw him would have thought that he was a man on the verge of giving up on life. The one thing that kept him moving however, was the thought of Agnes waiting for him.

He glanced behind him periodically, checking to see if he was being followed. Surely, the SIB men had noticed his absence by now, which meant the search for him would have commenced. However, the bushes were as still as the quiet night, save for the sounds of his rapid movements and loud gasps. The moon above was just a sliver, but it was bright enough to illuminate his path. Breathlessly, Francis forged ahead, wiping beads of sweat from his forehead. Finally, he noticed flames from a fire — the sign of a village.

He watched for a while before hesitantly emerging from the bushes. Though he was scared, he knew that if he remained where he was, he'd die from the fever that was rapidly taking hold of his body or from total blood loss. As he moved closer to the edge of the small village, he noticed a man and a woman sitting under a huge tree outside a small brick house. The sight caused a wave of nostalgia that enveloped Francis as the image of his own family home — which was just as small — appeared in his mind. The last time he'd been there was after Yaw's death. Running around the couple were three young kids, which made Francis think of Asantewaa. He realised he hadn't seen her for months. In fact, it felt like a decade since he'd seen any of his relatives.

Cautiously, Francis stumbled towards the happy family. He was hopeful that they wouldn't turn a severely injured man away. As he approached and as they noticed him, he could see the fear in the young woman's eyes. She quickly gathered the three kids and whispered something to them. They nodded and ran into the house. Francis experienced a brief moment of envy upon seeing the mother with her children. They were exactly the kind of family he craved for him and Agnes, but he doubted that it would ever happen, especially when considering his current predicament. He really had no idea if he'd make it out of this situation alive. Even if the soldiers didn't catch up with him, he'd probably die of fever.

The young man had remained motionless since Francis had approached, but suddenly, he jumped to his feet and walked boldly towards him. The man closely examined Francis who was surprised that there was no fear in his eyes.

"Who are you? Where are you coming from?" the man asked, while putting a protective arm around the woman's shoulders.

Glancing up at him, she said, "We should go in with the kids."

At that very moment, Francis's knees chose to buckle under him. He collapsed to the ground and groaned in pain. Aching all over, he felt like he'd had a rough tumble in a sack of rocks. How long he'd walked, he had no idea, but his body certainly told the tale. He was shaking even as he lay on the ground.

"We should help him," the man said.

Although consumed by pain, Francis realised that the couple were quietly arguing.

"What will we tell the children?" came the woman's wary voice.

That was the last thing Francis heard before he passed out.

* * *

He woke up the next morning on a makeshift bed in a dimly lit room. His pillow was made of piles of clothes stuffed together. His mouth tasted of sandpaper. He grimaced loudly at the pounding ache in his head. Then he slowly sat up. His eyes swept the room until they landed on the man he had met last night. Francis tried to jump to his feet, but he only succeeded in knocking over the glass of water at his feet.

"Relax," the man said. "What's your name?"

"Agyei," Francis lied, before quickly adding: "Thank you for helping me."

The man nodded and urged him to sit back down. "I had my wife tend to your wounds last night," he added. "But I can't help but wonder how you got them. Were you kidnapped?"

The question didn't surprise Francis at all; with the Rawlings regime, kidnappings and a host of other atrocities were no longer uncommon. He nodded, then explained how he'd escaped from the SIB. By the time he finished his account, the man's wife was in the room.

"Are you a soldier?" she blurted out.

The man instantly put a hand over her mouth. "You don't want the kids to hear that, Victoria," he admonished her. Then he turned to Francis. "You aren't a soldier, are you?" he asked.

In all his years of being in the army, Francis had never imagined that there might come a time when he'd have to publicly deny The Force. The army had been his life. It used to be his lifeline too. He had loved being a soldier but now circumstances beyond his control had changed everything, and as a result, he wasn't sure who he was anymore. In truth, he had wanted out for a long time, but he'd realised that he couldn't just simply leave the army, at least not by walking calmly out of the front door. Even though getting arrested and then escaping from prison had done the trick, of course, the risks involved were very high. Meanwhile, if word got out that the couple who'd welcomed him were housing a soldier and one on the run to boot, not only would he lose his life, but the innocent family would also be made to pay dearly.

"I'm not a soldier," Francis finally replied.

The couple exchanged a look that Francis knew meant that they did not believe him. Tears shimmered in Victoria's eyes, and clasping a hand over her mouth, she hurried out of the room. However, she was the least of Francis's problems right now. Nobody could find out about his stay in this house, soldier or no soldier. In fact, he made up his mind to exist like a ghost. The man sighed heavily and started to speak again.

"Please leave me alone," Francis begged him, averting his eyes.

But the man remained, standing and watching him closely.

"Why do you accept a complete stranger into your home?" Francis asked.

The man shrugged and gave him a tight smile. For the first time since Francis was a child, tears filled his eyes. He blinked furiously, willing away the embarrassing emotion, which was prompted by the kindness shown to him — a kindness he couldn't understand. As a soldier, he wasn't used to being warmly received by people. Usually, everyone was either scared of him or straight out hated him. He knew that he didn't deserve the couple's kindness. He'd killed people, strangers, without batting an eyelid. He'd never missed a shot either. The couple would have hated him and sent him away if they'd known the truth. So, he intended to keep up his lie for as long as possible. Plus, he knew from the terrain that the very next village was Tanoso, Agnes's village. Francis simply didn't want to imagine what would happen if he was recognised or news about his presence got out. He knew that he had to lay low for as long as he could.

"Please don't tell anyone I'm here," he pleaded with his host. "My survival is in your hands."

As the men spoke, Francis learnt that his saviour was Osei Appiah and he and his wife eventually agreed to shelter Francis, even though they knew he was likely a soldier. So Francis stayed. For the first few days, Victoria tiptoed around him and kept the kids away from his room, which he realised was actually a storeroom. Nevertheless, she remained polite and respectful at all times.

One evening, while the family of five were sitting outside under the moonlit sky, Francis, sitting in his bedroom just as he had been every day since his arrival, began to really ponder his fate. He had no idea what would become of him and he was desperate to see his Aggie and the rest of the family. How he was going to do that was something he could not work out. His injuries were already healing nicely with the wounds closing up, all thanks to Victoria who had administered some herbal medicine that she'd cooked up herself. However, his heart remained wounded. He'd served his nation with all his might and sweat and with everything he had, yet they'd turned against him in the blink of an eye. Now they wanted him dead because they were scared that he would highlight the crumbling state of Rawlings' government. He had no regrets about what he had done, but it had made him realise that all he actually wanted was to remain alive and see his wife. He was done risking his life for the betterment of the people because his antagonists had proven to him that it wasn't worth it.

His biggest fear in that moment was that he would not make it out alive. It didn't matter that he was innocent — they'd frame him for something just to justify their actions and tarnish his reputation. This thought, however, renewed his resolve because he knew the type of man that he was — a man who loved his country and his family. He had to stay alive for his family, to whom he had unwittingly brought so much trouble by joining the army. Then and there, he refused to let his decision cause them even more pain than they had already endured.

Later that night, Victoria entered his room. "I'll tend to your wounds now," she said, holding a bowl of herbal medicine in one hand and a small white napkin in the other.

Francis shook his head and took the items from her. "I can tend my own wounds," he insisted.

They played a silent battle of wills until the kids suddenly ran into the room and flocked around Victoria. They were all boys and exactly the same height, and two of them even had the same face. Francis stared at them in awe. It was at this point that he realised they were triplets. He'd never seen triplets before and wanted to ask Victoria how she was able to take care of three children of the same age all at once. Asantewaa alone was a handful when she was in the mood, but Francis knew it was nothing compared to three boys. As he'd realised since his arrival, the noise from their supposedly tiny lungs was enough to pull the roof down. He was yet to get properly acquainted with them, but he knew that Victoria didn't want that to happen, so he didn't engage with them. However, hiding behind their mother, they quietly examined him with big dark eyes.

"Is that one of our uncles?" one of them wanted to know, and Francis looked on in amusement as Victoria struggled to come up with a convincing answer.

When he'd finished applying the herbs to the sores on his legs, she picked up the bowl and napkin and shepherded the kids out of the room. Their murmurs continued down the hallway, and though Victoria told them to be quiet, they ignored her. Meanwhile, Francis stayed in his room and listened to them chatter incessantly as Osei also tried to calm them down, with little success. In fact, Francis only managed to sleep once the children slept. He couldn't complain though because his heart was filled with gratitude just to have a roof over his head; right now, that was all that mattered.

After seeing the Appiah triplets, he couldn't get the idea of having his own set out of his mind. In fact, with nothing else to do, his imaginings of what life could be with children took over his every waking moment. The desire to have his own children had been strong anyway, and he loved the idea of a close-knit family. He also knew though, that it would never happen unless he found a way to reach Agnes. In any event, it was better to think about something much more pleasant than his harrowing ordeal and the disappointment that life in the army had delivered to him. It was also a way to pass the slow days in what was essentially another version of confinement; that irony had not failed to pass him by, as well as how each version brought its own troubles.

About a week after he'd escaped from the SIB headquarters, a statewide search for Francis was launched. When Osei heard about this, he came into his guest's room after the kids were fast asleep. For the first time since Francis had come to live with them, Osei pulled out the rickety chair from the corner of the room and sat heavily on it. For a moment, Francis feared that it might collapse under him, but Osei remained seated even as the chair continued to creak. He looked at Francis, scoffed, and then looked at him again.

"It's you," he stated, plainly and simply. The blood had completely drained from his face.

Francis, ignorant of this latest development, asked him what was wrong.

"I went to watch my favourite football team play on TV at a café," Osei replied. "During the game, the transmission was abruptly interrupted for an emergency announcement where they showed a photo of you. Your face is also plastered all over the walls around here. In fact, it'll only be a matter of time before they put a bounty on your head. Is your name really Agyei?"

Francis had made up the name for fear of being ratted out. Now that his real name had been announced on national TV, it was only a matter of time before his luck with Osei ran out. However, instead of responding to his question, he asked, "Did you say anything to anyone?"

Osei looked at him like he was dense. "I've housed you and clothed you these past few days. What makes you think I'd be so vile as to expose a man in hiding? Besides, if I did, I'd be in trouble too."

Francis was relieved to hear this, but he remained nervous. It was possible that someone had seen him the night the Appiahs had taken him in. What would happen if that person now came out to expose him?

"Are you a soldier?" Osei asked.

Francis remained silent. He contemplated how much information was too much information. If he said anything, Victoria would certainly not have handled it as calmly as Osei. Women were known to be more emotional and he'd seen traits of intense vulnerability in her. As he thought about how to answer Osei, he realised that if he played his cards right, he could get information to his family without having to show himself. So, he begged Osei for a favour.

"Can you find my brother-in-law? Charles Peprah is his name. He's the assistant superintendent for the police force."

"I can't do that even if I wanted to," Osei replied. "There are soldiers everywhere and there is no way I am drawing attention to myself."

Over the next few days, Francis brought up the issue of finding Charles again and again, but the conversation always ended in disagreement. Meanwhile, he refused to reveal why he was being hunted because he was scared that if Osei knew, he would kick him out, or that Victoria would convince him to do so. Stepping out of the house would mean his immediate capture, not just because there were soldiers everywhere, but also because the latest development on the news was that a large bounty had been placed on his head. As much as Francis could trust Osei not to rat him out, he didn't trust the neighbours. Francis was left bound and frustrated. He spent days and nights worrying his head off; he was scared that he would never see his family again. They were the very reason he'd risked an escape from captivity, but now that one act appeared to have been in vain. It didn't seem right.

For days, he couldn't function properly, particularly as he was now having nightmares that woke him up frequently. He lay on the bed all day and left his food untouched, prompting Victoria to complain bitterly to Osei about Francis wasting their food. Life now held no meaning for him. He fantasised about how it would have been better to simply end everything in the SIB cell because there was no difference between being in that prison and the life he was currently living. It was now about four months since he had been arrested and since he had seen Agnes. Everything in between felt like one long, dark season, the kind that left him cut off from the world and from himself. Francis had no idea what was going on with the nation and its rulers. However, from what he had observed with the Appiahs, the economy appeared to be gradually looking up, even if it was still far from decent. The meals on their table had become a little more varied, rice and stew appearing more often instead of just plain gari, and clothes in the markets seemed easier to come by than before.

Unbeknownst to him, though, coup attempts on the government had become rampant. Around the time he'd escaped from the SIB headquarters, a coup to overthrow Rawlings and the PNDC had been plotted by Ghanaian dissidents along with eight American mercenaries; amongst them was also an Argentine. They'd boarded a ship called *MV Nobistor* in Brazilian territorial waters, with a plan to travel to Ghana with six tons of FAL rifles, submachine guns, hand grenades, revolvers and ammunition. However, the PNDC authorities had received intelligence about the planned coup and had alerted the Brazilian police, who'd arrested those on board. So, although Rawlings had entered politics with a gun, it increasingly seemed as if guns could not be used to remove him from power.

*　　*　　*

When Osei realised that Francis was persistent in his desire to find his brother-in-law, he eventually relented and decided to risk it. Without further delay, he headed to Tanoso, but for days, he couldn't locate Charles, as no one seemed to know him. Yet with soldiers controlling the streets, Osei could also sense the fear in those he asked. His search seemed fruitless. However, on his way back to Tanoso one evening, he was accosted by a man who appeared to be very interested in him. At first, Osei got scared, wondering if his life was in danger.

"Let's go for a drink," the man insisted.

Tired from his unsuccessful search, Osei welcomed the idea of a chilled drink, and as the man asked him questions, he revealed that someone he knew had instructed him to seek out his family. Eventually, the man revealed himself.

"… Well, I'm Charles."

Osei was greatly relieved to hear this, having feared that he may unwittingly have played into the hands of the army.

"Come back to my home with me," he suggested.

However, Charles refused. "Let's bide our time, because someone may be watching us," he said.

Charles had spent days observing this stranger who'd kept asking for him. Their family had stopped receiving news about Francis for a while, and knowing how the government worked, Charles suspected foul play. He was certain that Francis had been killed. So, when he'd heard about this stranger asking for him, he'd assumed it was just a ploy to trick him, which is why he'd remained undercover, silently watching Osei for several days. After having established that his fears were unfounded, he'd decided to show his face.

* * *

When Charles shared the news that Francis was alive and close by with his sister Agnes, she broke down in tears and wailed in relief.

"We have to leave this country immediately," she cried.

"Yes," Charles agreed. "Now that we know that he's alive, that'll be the best decision. However, I'll have to see him first to confirm that it's him."

Agnes begged to go with him but he refused. Having an emotional woman on the trip might draw unwanted attention that would have landed them both in trouble. So, instead, he took his time, waiting until he was certain that it was safe to go and visit Osei.

* * *

Francis initially believed Osei when he said that he'd found Charles, after a while though, he wasn't so sure anymore. Doubts crept in as Charles didn't turn up in the days and weeks after Osei's return. Francis had expected his brother-in-law to immediately show up and take him away. So, when Charles finally did show up, three weeks after Osei had found him, because Francis no longer had any expectations, he sat frozen in shock for a good minute.

He had never been close to his brother-in-law, but he'd chosen to seek him out because of his position in the police force. He knew that no matter what, Charles would try and find a way to help him out of his predicament. He also knew that by assisting someone who was wanted by the army, Charles was taking a huge risk. So for him to answer his call for help, Francis was very grateful. For the first time ever, he pulled Charles into a tight hug and wept like a baby on his shoulder. Questions upon questions about Agnes and Asantewaa spilled from his lips. When he got the reassurances he needed, he pulled back and sat down, crying some more, his heart filled with joy at the prospect of being with his family again.

8

"Agnes will be elated," Charles said. Even though Francis had lost a ton of weight from his time in prison and his subsequent lonely stay with strangers, Charles knew that Agnes would be most grateful to finally see her husband again. Before they went to her, the two brothers-in-law spent several hours together, so Francis could share details about his escape.

Although Charles applauded his bravery, he didn't like the risk he'd taken. Francis understood that his concern was down to the fact that he didn't want to endanger Agnes. Of course, neither did Francis, but his only wish was that he could be with her. It was pretty obvious that his career in the army was over, so all he had left was Agnes.

"There are too many eyes watching us," Charles cautioned. "Tanoso is simply too close to the SIB headquarters, so it's best if you move away from here before reuniting with her. Otherwise, you'll most certainly be caught."

Disheartened, Francis accepted his rationale, especially considering that Osei had gone round the villages asking for Charles. Before Charles left that evening, he promised to return with a solution to relocate Francis.

"Lay low until then," he advised Francis.

After Charles was gone, Osei and Victoria came to Francis's room. The hurt Victoria felt was clearly expressed on her face. She barraged him for lying to them even as they had opened their home to him. Osei shocked himself when he realised the risk he'd unknowingly exposed his family to. Though they didn't give voice to their desire for him to leave, Francis knew that he had overstayed his welcome. All he could do was beg for their forgiveness.

* * *

At around ten o'clock in the evening on 31 May 1986, one month since his first visit, Charles returned to see Francis with a plan. He wanted to sneak him out in the dead of night, so they'd have the cover of darkness on their side. No one had time to even debate the plan, but as they made to leave, Osei stopped them.

"It's too risky for him to go out like that," he warned them. "The soldiers are more active and alert at night. I've seen them when I've been out to watch football games. Francis needs a disguise."

Charles agreed so Victoria gave Francis one of her dark niqabs, which covered the entire body, including the lower part of the face. Francis laughed at first but then put it on. Looking every inch the everyday Muslim woman, he left the Appiah's house with his brother-in-law.

On their walk, Francis realised that Charles was heading towards the West Akim Municipal District in the eastern part of southern Ghana and away from Tanoso. He'd been to the area on an official army-related visit, so he was quite familiar with the terrain. Francis didn't know what Charles' plan was, but he couldn't ask him; they had to remain silent since they didn't know who was within earshot. They passed half a dozen burning fires on their way, signs that the soldiers had been terrorising the area. When they came to a roadblock, they were harassed by a bunch of soldiers.

"Pull off your niqab so we can confirm your identity," one of them hissed.

"According to our religion, my wife is not allowed to show her face in public,"

Charles quickly replied, while Francis remained silent so that his voice wouldn't betray him.

"Why are you travelling so late at night?" another soldier asked.

"Because my wife is very sick and needs the attention of a herbalist," Charles said.

The soldiers eyed them sceptically and shone their bright torches directly in their faces. Throughout the tense exchange, Charles didn't change his story, and neither did he reveal that he was a police officer, knowing that this information was likely to open up a can of worms, with further questions potentially leading to Francis being exposed. Eventually, after much deliberation amongst themselves, the soldiers let them go.

When they arrived in Asamankese, a town on the main highway to Ghana's second largest city, Kumasi, Charles led the way to a small bar.

"Why are we here?" Francis asked him.

"Because I have a friend here in Asamankese, and it would be safer for you to stay with him until I've sorted out the ticket and passport for your trip to the UK."

It had been so long since Francis had heard about the potential trip to the UK that he was left confused for a few seconds. He'd thought Agnes and her sisters would have given up on those travel plans, especially since he had disappeared for such a long time. The idea of staying with another stranger didn't appeal to him. He wanted to be outside in the sun so that it would rejuvenate his spirit. At that moment, he felt exhausted both physically and mentally, burnt out by the constant running and hiding. Yet he also realised that going back to Agnes, like he wanted to, would only pose more problems for them. So, he reluctantly agreed to Charles' plan.

"You'll get your freedom soon," Charles promised. "When you're out of Ghana and in the UK."

The knowledge that Agnes knew he was alive didn't ease how much Francis missed her. In fact, it made him want her more. He thought about her and Asantewaa every waking moment, and if being with them meant that they would have to leave Ghana for good, then so it would be. They would just have to build a new life there in the UK. The idea of leaving his mother and the rest of his family, as well as everything else he'd ever known, was a bitter pill to swallow. He'd always imagined that it would take him quite a while to actually decide whether he was going to move, but now, the decision had been taken out of his hands. The situation had robbed him of any say. It was the UK or back to prison and possible execution. The army never forgave, and he wasn't expecting his case to be any different.

Yet, for the first time since he'd become a soldier all those years ago, he was genuinely glad to be given a chance to leave the army behind. It was an unstable life as the Rawlings government had made the army ugly and undesirable. Francis had done things he never thought he'd do and taken up roles in the government that had constantly pricked at his conscience. He was also painfully aware that not every prison escapee was as lucky as he was. Which is why, there and then, he made up his mind to seize this opportunity that his wife's family had bestowed upon him. So, he started to look at the positive aspects of his situation and especially the bright future that awaited him and Agnes in the UK. Before he got there though, there was this stop coming up in Asamankese.

His host there was called Mensah. He was a simple farmer and a former police officer who'd retired early as a result of an injured leg. Mensah was a man of few words, but the conversations they did have were mostly about politics, meaning Francis was able to voice his frustrations with the PNDC government. Their interactions made him feel lighter and momentarily lessened the heavy burden that remained on his shoulders.

* * *

Meanwhile, though Agnes knew where he was, she couldn't risk visiting him given that the army had spies everywhere. Instead, Charles acted as a messenger between them. Sometimes, instead of a letter professing her undying love for him, Francis received a large basket of homemade food especially prepared for him.

A few weeks after his arrival at Mensah's home, Charles brought some awful news. Asantewaa was terribly sick and Agnes was spending every waking moment caring for the little girl. After hearing this, Francis became withdrawn. He had received a letter from Agnes a few days earlier, but she hadn't mentioned this development at all. Clearly, she'd deliberately kept that information from him because she didn't want him to worry. That realisation made him feel useless. Part of his reason for joining the army had been that he and his family would earn the respect that would be attached to his name. It also meant that he'd be able to protect them. So, in this situation now, he felt like a failure. As it was, he couldn't even protect himself while his wife was being harassed by the same army that he'd served in.

He admitted to himself that his parents might have been right. They'd known what he was getting into by joining the army. Being so young and blinded by his desire to be a soldier, he hadn't been able to see the reality of what a life in the army would mean. He wished he could turn back the hands of time and not send the letter to the government that had started all this mess. His life and that of his family might have turned out differently. It might not have been perfect, but at least he would have been with his family and have his freedom. However, because of his actions, he was slowly losing who he was — the head of his home. The protector. Instead, he was a nobody. His wife couldn't even confide in him anymore.

* * *

As the days turned into weeks, he gradually became both physically and mentally exhausted by being cooped up indoors with nothing to do. So, when Mensah went to his farm, Francis would put on a big straw hat and dark shades to disguise himself and stroll to the market. The bustle amid the vendors and shoppers made him feel alive again. Until he ran into Charles.

"What do you think you're doing?" Charles asked sharply, as he pulled Francis into a dark alley.

The sun was very hot that day. Francis was sweating heavily under his black outfit and at that moment, even more so from the shock of being recognised in his disguise. He'd thought he had got away with it.

"I can smell you from a mile away," Charles said angrily. "Are you trying to jeopardise the travel plans and get arrested?" He stepped away for a moment and scanned up and down the street.

"I didn't see any soldiers at all during my walk," Francis defended himself.

This claim didn't sit well with Charles. To make this worse, Francis repeated the misdemeanour days later, and when Charles caught him the second time, he went straight to Agnes. Consequently, a few days later, Francis received a very harsh letter from her. Agnes didn't mince her words as she pleaded with him to keep himself alive for her. Francis was thoroughly warned against pulling a similar stunt and endangering his life.

Yet, as much as the letter shook Francis, it also made him sceptical about their planned trip to the UK. He started to worry deeply about getting caught alongside Agnes, aware that she'd be implicated. He was also certain that the army would be looking out for him at the airport. He communicated his growing concerns to Charles, who, in turn, shared their conversation with his family. As a result, they decided that Francis and Agnes would travel to the UK separately. Agnes didn't like the idea though. She wanted to be with Francis as soon as possible and waiting to get to the UK before that could happen seemed far too long a time to wait. Their tickets and passports were still being prepared. She wasn't even sure they'd actually get the approval they needed, so it sounded to her like she might never see her husband again.

Her anxiety about the situation worsened daily until it made her ill. Thankfully, by then, Asantewaa was better. At first, everyone thought it was the constant worry that had consumed Agnes, and so they focussed on reassuring and encouraging her. However, she continued to deteriorate so much that one day, her mother declared that she should go to hospital. As it turned out, she was moved from hospital to hospital and from herbalist to herbalist, but nothing seemed to help. When Francis heard about her ill health, he begged Mensah to assist him in getting some special herbs. Fortunately, Mensah obliged because he could see how distressed Francis was. They both went under the cover of darkness using a torch and fortunately managed to get all the ingredients he needed to mix a herbal treatment for Agnes, just the way he'd learned from his father.

After a few days of religiously taking the herbal medicine that her husband had painstakingly formulated, Agnes recovered completely. It was like a miracle, a miracle that only Francis could have pulled off. He was overjoyed when the message had been relayed to him. The experience reminded him of his herbal prowess and how his life could've turned out very differently had he become a herbalist. On the other hand, he might not have met Agnes without his army uniform. So, no matter how everything else had panned out, he had one thing to be grateful for, and that was Agnes. She was his all, and without her, his life would've been a very dark place.

Meanwhile, Agnes fought back the regrets that threatened to rear their ugly head every time she thought of Francis. Everyone had warned her, but she'd thought they could fly across the sky without wings. She didn't understand how everything had gone so wrong and how they were suddenly running for their lives. She blamed it on Rawlings' government, which, she said, had ruined the peaceful lives of millions of Ghanaians.

However, not everyone across the country shared that view. Just as Jerry Rawlings was a saviour to some, he was a devil to others. He was called 'Junior Jesus' by masses of students, workers and soldiers that saw him as a moral crusader who understood their hunger and frustrations. To them, he remained a hero. Rawlings' point was that he was merely struggling to contain the more violent elements of his revolution and his supporters celebrated him for recognising their humanity and saving the nation from indiscipline. Those who subscribed to that view also claimed that he was ultimately a strategic pragmatist whose use of military discipline saved Ghana from catastrophic civil wars like those seen in Nigeria and Liberia.

By contrast, Agnes and others called him 'Junior Judas' and accused him of betraying his supporters and setting the country back. Relatives and friends of those who'd been killed, detained or tortured in various revolts continued to hold Rawlings responsible for the vindictiveness of his soldiers. Meanwhile, many children not only had to endure hearing about their parents' death in the press, but they also had to look on as the nation celebrated.

Every day the country seemed to lurch from one chaotic situation after another, and stuck in Mensah's home, Francis got so fed up that he stopped watching the news altogether. Once more, the idea of leaving Ghana became very appealing to him.

* * *

Once the turmoil of Agnes's illness was over, Charles decided that it was time to bring Francis' family into the fold. For the three months that Francis had been in hiding with Mensah, The Oppongs had remained in the dark about what had happened to him. It didn't take long to get the clan together as they had remained anxious about the whereabouts of their brother. When Charles gathered the clan in their family home in Kuntanse, the majority of Francis' siblings sat directly opposite him in the family living room, and looking at them, Charles briefly wondered how the universe had kept them all together.

Charles' parents also had twelve children, with Agnes being the youngest. However, over several years, even before Agnes was born, four of them had died. He was struck by how blessed The Oppongs were to still have each other. Charles had to yank himself out of his reverie when he glanced at Afia and saw the fear and worry etched across her face; he refocused his mind to the matter at hand.

When Afia heard that Francis was alive, she fell to her knees on the stone floor.

"Yaw, your son is alive," she cried out loud, tears streaming down her cheeks.

The mood changed however, when Charles told them about the plans for Francis and Agnes to travel to the UK;

Afia didn't like it one bit. She clearly stated her fear of foreigners and how they'd be mean to her son. That was not the kind of life for any of her children, no matter how promising it looked. She didn't necessarily mind if Francis remained in hiding; all she cared about was that he was reachable. By contrast, if he was in another country, he might as well have been on another unknown planet.

George, although he'd never been abroad, tried to reassure his mother. He was certain that his in-laws wouldn't lead Francis into danger, especially as Agnes would be going along too. Meanwhile, Akua Biaa sided with Afia. She thought it was too risky for her little brother to escape Ghana since he was being hunted by the army and the government. So, she expressively suggested that he remain in hiding for as long as he was alive. However, the rest of the siblings countered this suggestion, pointing out that it would be a meaningless life, especially for someone who'd played such an active role in the army.

After the meeting, Charles returned to his family with mixed feelings. He'd been so sure, that getting Francis to escape to the UK was the best option. Yet, having heard Afia's worries, he wondered whether or not he had the right to take a child from its mother. His two sisters who lived in the UK had the full support of their family. But The Oppongs' differing opinions confused him. When he told Agnes what had transpired, she laughed.

"I feel exactly the same way as Afia and Akua Biaa. I'm only trying to put on a strong front for Francis, but it's very hard for me too."

So, undeterred, they stepped up their preparations for the trip to the UK. With his connections, Charles was able to pull some strings, and by 18 August 1986, the plane tickets as well as their passports were ready. Another month passed before it was the eve of Agnes'ss departure. Her family were overjoyed, yet she was apprehensive about travelling without Francis. She was scared for him. Agnes desperately wanted to start a new life in the UK with her husband, but she was on edge because there was a possibility that he might get caught and she'd never see him again. That night before her trip, she cried herself to sleep wishing that she could hold Francis' hand and walk into the airport with him. However, she also knew that if she did that, it could lead them into even more trouble.

The next day, with her fingers tightly clinging to Asantewaa's hand, Agnes walked towards the departure gate at the airport. It had been an emotional goodbye with her family, especially as Charles had advised against everyone accompanying her to the airport. He was her sole companion. As she sat waiting for the announcement to board, in her mind, there were many scenarios where she and Asantewaa were captured and taken away. Fear like none she'd ever experienced before seized her and wouldn't let go until she and Asantewaa were walking onto the plane. It was a wild and exhilarating moment for Agnes and pushing every negative thought to the back of her mind, she looked forward to a bright future in a strange land.

* * *

A week later, it was Francis's turn to travel. Once again, he wore a disguise. Meanwhile, Charles pulled some more strings and got a police jeep to take Francis to Accra. On 26 September 1986, more than six months after he'd escaped from the SIB headquarters, Francis, wearing a niqab, was driven across the tarmac at the airport, past the security agents. The following day, he landed in the UK.

Agnes and one of her sisters, Adwoa Badu, who everyone called Adwoa, were waiting for him at Heathrow Airport. His heart threatened to explode in his chest when he saw his wife for the first time in nearly a year. Agnes's eyes were red and filled with tears. Just as he drew closer, Asantewaa came out from hiding and jumped into his arms. Francis was so relieved, for he'd thought she would've forgotten about him by now. He pulled Agnes into a tight hug, and with both of them in his arms, he felt like he had finally come home.

9

It turned out that Francis and Agnes would live, not with Adwoa, but with Afriyie, who was around 16 years older than Agnes. She was a midwife and lived in Streatham, a bustling South London neighbourhood with a growing West African community. Francis counted himself very lucky and privileged that she so readily accepted him and Agnes into her home. The neighbours also welcomed them with open arms to the point that it felt as if they had all known each other from back home. Most were from other African countries, which was why they could easily relate to them. Everyone's accommodating attitude put Francis at ease, especially as he was the only person without a blood relative in England; Agnes was the only one he could really call family.

This was Agnes's first time travelling outside of Ghana. Francis, on the other hand, had travelled extensively during his time in the army, so stepping into a new country wasn't new to him. However, seeing Agnes's excitement as they visited the sights in the city like Buckingham Palace and Trafalgar Square, marvelling at the clean streets and bright shopfronts, filled him with quiet joy. Though it was cold, they both had a sense that London was full of possibility.

The early days at Afriyie's were comfortable. Agnes made herself useful by helping around the house, cleaning and cooking. She also visited Adwoa and spent time with Asantewaa; Asantewaa had moved in with her mother pretty much as soon as Agnes and Francis had arrived. Despite that, Asantewaa still called Agnes 'Mummy' when she visited; Agnes didn't mind what Asantewaa called her. She'd practically raised the little girl as her own, though she couldn't wait to give birth to her own. It was a yearning that grew stronger by the day and it pained her that she didn't have children as yet. It was only Asantewaa's presence in her life that dulled the ache. The little girl had brought so much joy to her life, especially at a time when she'd been alone and desperate. Asantewaa had filled the void that Francis had left when he'd been in prison and over the months after his disappearance.

For Francis, his first few days in London weren't exactly what he'd expected as his sleeping pattern was a complete mess. During the day, he would be fast asleep, only to lie wide awake at night. The time difference between Ghana and London was merely an hour, so he wasn't sure why he was so restless. Agnes revealed that she'd experienced exactly the same upon her arrival in the UK a week earlier.

"I think it's just the change of environment," she reassured him.

This included the weather in London in late September, which was unlike anything they knew in Ghana. Summer had come to an end and autumn was in the air, which meant that regardless of how sunny it was, Agnes could feel a chill in her bones. Afriyie had heaters in her house, but they did next to nothing to warm Agnes. In the end, Afriyie gave Agnes a woollen jacket, which Agnes wore day in and day out, even though she still felt cold. Francis' time in the army again came in handy. He quickly adapted to the frigid temperatures and so was comfortable with the weather. The temperature was the least of his concerns, though. Every day he marvelled at how he had escaped Ghana and its troubles. With Agnes by his side, he was fulfilled.

"How do you cope in this weather with no shirt on?" Agnes asked him as he sat cross-legged on the couch munching on a piece of muffin that one of the neighbours had brought them.

"You forget that I'm a soldier, Aggie," he replied. "But don't worry, you will also get used to the weather soon."

"I don't think I will, Kojo," she sighed, and they shared a laugh while she wiped the TV shelf with a small white rag.

The days in London passed by swiftly. In the blink of an eye, Francis had been in London for a full week. A complete week with his wife. He couldn't believe his luck. At the beginning of the year, stuck in the SIB prison, he'd thought that his end had come. He'd even given up on seeing sunlight again, and he certainly had no idea that his life would take such a dramatic turn. Now, Francis was grateful for the help from his in-laws and had expressed his gratitude to Afriyie and Adwoa daily since his arrival. Though completely bored out of his mind from staying at home all day, he couldn't have asked for anything more. Being removed from the troubles in Ghana was all that mattered for now, and he was willing to ride the tide until it was time to start rebuilding their lives.

* * *

About three weeks into the couple's arrival, Afriyie decided to host a little welcome party for Francis and Agnes. Francis was touched, and both were excited and looking forward to it. It had been a long time since they had celebrated anything. Afriyie went all out, decorating the house and getting all the right ingredients to make traditional Ghanaian dishes, as well some international ones that were new to Francis and Agnes. Adwoa and Agnes helped with the cooking, and the sisters enjoyed reminiscing about their childhood as they did so. Afriyie invited most of her friends and some of her colleagues to meet her little sister and brother-in-law. As they trickled in one by one, in couples, families and groups, they too showed their excitement to meet the new arrivals.

The guests devoured the delicious food with gusto; it was almost as if they'd never eaten before. Francis realised that no matter where one was in the world, free food never went unappreciated. It was a slightly different experience for Agnes who was hesitant to try some of the dishes she'd never had before. However, with encouragement from the guests, she tasted some and actually liked them. Unlike his wife, Francis was all up in the food. Being a soldier, he was used to different dishes, including the unpalatable, but the food that Afriyie had prepared was like nothing he had ever eaten before. He thoroughly enjoyed those that were unfamiliar to his palate.

Francis' initial fear of being treated differently turned out to be unfounded. Even Afriyie's white friends were welcoming. They weren't snobbish like he'd expected. However, Francis suspected that Afriyie must have carefully selected them. He spoke with nearly everyone and for the first time in a long while, he enjoyed himself without glancing behind him, scared that someone might be watching. Gone were the nights of sleeping with one eye open and the days of working under the brutal command of another. The fear of being executed had followed him the entire time he was in prison, up until the very moment he'd stepped foot on British soil at Heathrow. Now, it was finally gone, and in its place was genuine peace. His wife was with him; it was the definition of the perfect life for Francis. He was free at last.

He'd also never seen Agnes so happy, and her happiness doubled his own excitement. He pulled her into his arms for a dance, thrilled that everything was going so well, with Afriyie making him feel like family and ensuring that they had all that they needed. Francis was grateful for everything. After the uncertainty they'd left behind in Ghana, simply having a roof over their heads and the safety of family was enough.

10

After nearly a year of the three living together, Afriyie entered a serious relationship. Not long after, her partner moved in. As a result, space was tight. Four adults in a small house left little room for privacy, and both Agnes and Francis started to feel like intruders. Afriyie never made them feel unwelcome, though. It was out of respect for her new relationship that Agnes approached Adwoa to ask if they could move in with her. At that time, Adwoa still lived alone with Asantewaa, so without hesitation, she agreed.

Francis and Agnes moved into Adwoa's flat in a high-rise block in Stockwell. Once again, they were grateful to be taken in. The space was quieter, and at first, the adjustment was smooth. Agnes and her sister rekindled a bond they hadn't felt in years, and Francis tried to settle into a routine. Underneath the surface though, things began to shift.

Within a few weeks of having moved to the UK, the novelty had started to wear off, and both Agnes and Francis had begun to feel the weight of idleness. Now, a year later and still not working the feeling was unbearable. Francis was used to structure, and movement from his years in the military and led a very active life as a soldier both at work and socially. Although he'd enjoyed the perks of relaxing for a while, it felt like he was losing his sense of purpose. Agnes was also just as restless. She longed to contribute, to feel useful, to build something of her own.

When they'd talked about moving to London, being unemployed was something they had never considered. Francis had looked forward to getting a job and earning his keep and more. He also knew that his mum and siblings were eager for him to make it big in London and send them money; it was expected of him. When Francis broached the subject with Agnes, she was in agreement.

"I want to work too," she said.

Although Agnes had not worked back in Ghana, she'd often accompanied her older sister to the farm. And like Francis, she was exhausted from being cooped up in Adwoa' home.

By then, Asantewaa was enrolled in school, and Adwoa, who worked as platform staff at a nearby British Rail station, had instructed Francis and Agnes not to venture outside. She told them that, as they did not have the right papers to be in the country, they could get into trouble if the police saw them. Francis didn't quite believe Adwoa, but he let the matter slide. So, when Agnes suggested they ask her for help to get a job, he doubted that she would help them. However, on the other hand, he could no longer tolerate his idleness; it was driving him crazy. In the end, he decided that whether Adwoa would help them or not, she had to know of their plight.

* * *

One night while her sister was resting in the living room after work, Agnes broached the subject.

"We've been thinking," Agnes said, "maybe it's time we found some work."

Adwoa laughed. "Work? Do you know what it takes to work in this country?" she scoffed. "You don't have the papers. You're illegal here. If you're caught, you'll be deported."

Francis tried to reason with her, thanking her for everything she'd done and gently explaining that they weren't ungrateful, just tired of doing nothing. Regardless, Adwoa completely dismissed the idea. When Agnes offered that perhaps she could put in a word at her workplace, Adwoa immediately shut it down and even laughed at the idea of her baby sister working. Agnes wasn't too upset about Adwoa underestimating her capabilities; she was more disturbed by her reluctance to help Francis. She couldn't understand why her sister didn't want him to earn money. Adwoa knew perfectly well that he had come to the UK in search of a better life and discouraging him from getting a job was like clipping the wings of a bird. While the troubles in Ghana had hastened Francis' decision to travel with her, Agnes had also promised him that she would get him a job in the UK through her sisters.

So now, as she noticed the tight clench of his jaw and the sharpness of his eyes as they darted between her and Adwoa, she felt like she had failed her husband. As Adwoa excused herself and left with Asantewaa sleeping in her arms, Agnes felt like she was looking at a stranger. The Adwoa she'd known while growing up had been different — kind, loving and easy-going — the exact opposite of what she had become.

Adwoa had grown bitter and resentful after getting pregnant at the age of 19. Their mother had welcomed the pregnancy with open arms despite Adwoa not being married. However, the situation had changed Agnes's sister, who'd suddenly become a shell of herself, easily angered and only loving to those she could benefit from. Asantewaa's father had tried to remain in the child's life, but Adwoa had completely shut him out and outright refused to have anything to do with him. In fact, she had completely banned him from seeing Asantewaa or getting close to his daughter in any way. Her family suspected that Adwoa couldn't stand his financial instability — he was too poor for her taste. She'd been with him because she'd loved him, but when she'd given birth and realised that he couldn't even spare a penny for their baby, she'd grown angry, hating herself for associating with someone so irresponsible and incapable. Adwoa had always been lively and wanted a good life. She'd craved more for herself than the parochial life of a village girl and had wanted to explore the world. Now saddled with a baby, her dreams had suddenly appeared unattainable. When the opportunity to leave Ghana had come up, she had seized it without looking back. Agnes had hoped the change in environment would soothe her sister's raw nerves, but it was obvious that the wounds from her unexpected pregnancy still ran deep.

When days turned into weeks and Adwoa kept ignoring their request for help, Agnes decided to confide in Afriyie. Much to Agnes's surprise, her big sister was very eager to help and commended them for their desire to work.

"Leave everything to me," she said.

When Agnes told Francis about Afriyie's willingness to help them, he couldn't believe his ears. He pinched himself just to be sure that he wasn't dreaming.

"So, why did Adwoa claim that we couldn't work here, then?" he wondered.

However, Agnes just laughed it off; her main concern was that at least one of her sisters were on board with their plan. One sister had shut the door, but another had opened a window, and that, for now, was enough.

11

As promised, within a few days, Afriyie managed to get Agnes and Francis each hooked up with a cleaning job at Heathrow Airport. The catch was that they had to use different names. Adwoa was right; they couldn't work in the UK under their real names because they didn't have the required papers. However, there was a way around it, which was using fake identities.

Francis' new name was Charles Nimako, the name of Agnes's older brother and Francis' saviour in Ghana. It was perfect because Charles had actually been to the UK and even studied in London. Meanwhile, Agnes retained her first name, but her surname also became Nimako. When his new identity card was placed in his palm, the reality of what it meant hit Francis hard. Throughout his life, he'd never expected that there might come a day when he would have to deny his name and heritage. He wondered what his family would think when they heard that he'd ditched his name for someone else's. The thin letters on the card seemed to mock him. He'd thought he was going to make a name for himself in London, but apparently, he was now going to have to do it using someone else's identity.

When the couple told Adwoa about their jobs, she mumbled her congratulations but warned them to be very cautious.

"The streets of London are teeming with policemen looking to sniff out immigrants," she said.

Her warning rang in Francis' ears. Paranoia got hold of him as he sat heavily on the bed the night before his first day at work. What would happen if the police uncovered his deception? Would he be thrown in jail here too? He certainly had no plans of going back to prison. Agnes, unaware of his misgivings, gathered the hem of her ankle-length dress and danced around their small bedroom. Her face was aglow with the excitement of finally being able to work and make money in the UK. She was on top of the world. Thankfully, her happiness was infectious, because soon, the same excitement bubbled up in Francis. He pushed his fears to the back of his mind because at the end of the day, they had no other option.

* * *

Their first day of work started off brilliantly. To wish them well, Adwoa gave them a lift, and after dropping them off, she herself headed off to work. As she drove off, Francis and Agnes stood alone in front of Heathrow. A few minutes later, a uniformed white man approached and led them into the terminal building.

When Francis had arrived in the UK, he hadn't cared about what the airport looked like — seeing his wife again had been his sole priority. Now, as he tightly clasped Agnes's hand and walked into the huge building with her, he let his eyes wander and appreciate his surroundings. Everything was bright and beautiful, and for the first time since he'd received his identity card, his worries lessened as his excitement to finally get to work prevailed. The man led them towards the restrooms, where he gave them instructions on what to do and handed them mops and buckets before leaving again.

"You seem quite eager," Agnes said to her husband.

"Aggie. I've been idle for too long," Francis replied.

As expected of public toilets, some of them were pretty messed up, but it didn't deter Francis. He'd seen worse as a soldier. Besides, Afriyie had obviously pulled some strings to get them their jobs, so he didn't want to disappoint her by shrinking from the task. His only worry was Agnes; he wasn't sure how she'd handle the job. They got through their first day smoothly and soon it was the end of their shift. The train journey home gave Agnes her first real sense of London after over a year in the city. The rumble of double-decker buses, the crisp air, and the bustling streets filled with market stalls and chatter hit all her senses. Francis noticed her wide-eyed excitement and smiled quietly; though he had travelled before, seeing Agnes taking it all in made the city feel new again.

After they arrived home, washed and settled in for the evening, Francis expressed his concerns to Agnes.

He wanted her to know that if the work was too much for her, she didn't have to continue. Agnes insisted that she was fine. He didn't believe her, but he also knew that nothing he said would dissuade her. She was determined to work, and nothing — not even her husband — was going to stop her.

* * *

Francis was very easy-going and, in many ways, a bit of a socialite. He'd always been able to win over pretty much anyone, from any background, with his quiet charm. True to form, after his shifts, he'd often hang around the airport chatting with travellers and staff alike, sharing snippets of their lives. It was through this casual though deliberate networking that he managed to get multiple additional jobs to bring in a little more money than his daily two-hour shift at Heathrow did. It meant that he was soon working ten hours a day. That was a big achievement for him.

He would get home several hours after Agnes, usually exhausted, but that was fine. It was nothing compared to army life, and he most certainly wasn't a lazy man. At least with cleaning, he knew what to expect: a hard day's work and a warm meal in the evening. As a soldier, it was backbreaking work, and they could go for days and even weeks without a decent meal. Francis was content. Now that progress had started, he knew he could conquer the world with Agnes by his side.

In just two months, money started coming in. Francis was thrilled. It seemed surreal; they were both paid the minimum wage but when multiplied by the at least five other jobs he'd managed to squeeze in, they were making a substantial amount. Bedtime became filled with animated talk about buying a house and a car. Agnes wanted a white house with a lawn and a white picket fence; Francis wanted a Mercedes-Benz. Although their combined earnings weren't enough to fulfil either of these wishes just yet, it didn't stop them from fantasising.

Agnes suggested that perhaps they could get married in a registry office to officially document their marriage on paper. An added bonus in that scenario was that she'd get to wear a beautiful white dress. It was an idea that Francis strongly considered because he had always pictured her radiant in a wedding dress. It was too soon though; first, they had to save up a bit more. After all, they couldn't bank on Adwoa feeding and housing them forever. At some point, they would have to find their own home. Then, they had other expenses, not least the fact that he sent money home to his siblings and ageing mum as often as he could. He had no idea when he'd return to Ghana, and he wanted to make sure that his family were financially stable.

* * *

About six months after starting at Heathrow, Francis, now more confident, got another cleaning job at Elephant and Castle Underground station. He earned more there, and everyone at the station loved him. The traits he'd developed as a soldier — the very ones that had made him who he was — also made him stand out. In particular, he was equally respectful to his colleagues, managers and passengers. Soon, he developed a friendship with his manager, Mr George, who had taken a genuine interest in him because of the fact that he stood apart from the rest of his staff.

Mr George was perhaps in his early 50s and was originally from St Lucia. He took Francis under his wing, adopting the role of big brother. It was the first time that Francis had developed a close friendship with someone from the Caribbean, and through him, had learnt much about the life of the black community in London. Mr George claimed that since Francis had started working at the station, there had been a lot of return customers and an increase in ticket sales. In his eyes, Francis could do no wrong, and in fact, he also recognised that Francis was capable of much more. He praised him for his unwavering work ethic and gradually advised and encouraged him to look into becoming a train engineer, especially as the pay was much better.

Francis had never operated or driven anything before; he had not even been on a bicycle. As the advice came from Mr George, whom he held in high esteem, he decided to apply for the role. It had taken him several weeks to make the decision, but he was determined to make Mr George proud as well as better himself.

* * *

On the night before he put in his application, Francis couldn't sleep as he had been particularly overwhelmed by what he was about to do. He had taken the cleaning jobs as a sure means of earning money. Of course he wanted to be part of a profession of some sort, but he had never thought too much about what he would do. Becoming a train driver was certainly not something he had even considered though. He thought about the change in his status that would come with driving a train, but it didn't blind him to the risks involved. He could crash; he could lose his life; he could cause others to lose their lives.

"What's wrong, Kojo?" Agnes asked him, as he kept twisting and turning in bed.

Francis explained. Agnes was surprised at his hesitation but did not feed his anxieties.

"I trust you, and I know you can do anything you put your mind to," she said.

Agnes's words ignited something in Francis. The fact that she believed in him wholeheartedly calmed him, and in that moment, he knew he could do it.

* * *

The following morning, Mr George escorted Francis to meet the Head of Operations of the London Underground.

"Here's the chap I told you about." That was how Mr George introduced Francis to the operations manager who was a tall and lanky man with another of those accents that Francis could not place. Mr George then excused himself, saying he'd see Francis later at the station.

The manager introduced himself as Simon McFadden, and the name alone told Francis that he was Scottish; the accent then made sense to him. As Mr McFadden asked Francis about his background and previous experience, inevitably, he learned that Francis had never driven anything at all. Rather than trying to dissuade him, he encouraged him further.

"There are hundreds of people who apply to be a train engineer every year, but very few are willing to put in the hard work," he said. "I hope you'll be among the few."

Indeed, Francis was willing to do whatever it took. Being a soldier had made him tough and resilient. Giving up wasn't part of his DNA, and neither was there room for failure.

"Right. Let's get down to business. Here are some forms you need to fill in. I'll show you where you can sit down to do that. Take your time."

It did take some time indeed to complete the forms. After he'd submitted them to Mr McFadden, he was told that he could start his training pretty much straight away. All that was needed to do was hand Francis over to his tutor and they would discuss the training schedule. As it turned out, the tutor was already waiting to meet him outside Mr McFadden's office. Francis was still in awe of how quickly things moved in London. If he had been in Ghana, in the same situation, he was sure that he would have been told to come back another day, a day unknown, to get started, if he got started in the current lifetime at all.

The driver assigned to train him was a jovial, round man called Bernard Shaw — Bernie for short. He immediately started showing Francis the ropes, starting with a tour of the train and a demonstration of the controls. This took the best part of an hour, and it was one of the most exhilarating hours Francis had spent since arriving in the city. The experience motivated him tremendously, and he could now see how he might build a life for himself, Agnes, and their future family. At the end of that first session, Bernie handed Francis his training schedule and manual and bade him farewell with a hearty, 'See you tomorrow!'

As it turned out, Bernie was the most patient man Francis had ever met. He spoke calmly and never shouted, even when he had to correct Francis multiple times. Fortunately, Francis was a fast learner, and in a little over three months, he'd mastered the basics as well as the technicalities involved in operating a train. Bernie told him that at the rate he was going, he could be ready for his test in another three months. This took Francis by surprise; he couldn't believe that he could be operating such big and complicated machine so soon. Despite his initial apprehension, he recommitted to applying himself even more so that he was ready when the time came.

* * *

As it turned out, Francis was indeed ready when the time came. Around seven months after his first training session, in December 1988, he passed the assessment test with flying colours. It was a gruelling two hours of practical tests, written questions and an oral examination. Mr George was beside himself with pride, and over the moon for his protegee. Francis himself was overjoyed, and the vision of a prosperous life in London had become clearer. He didn't even care that he would still have to wait for a position as an engineer to become available before he could use his new qualification. What mattered was that he had a new skill and had proved to himself that he could be more than a soldier.

About a week after passing the test, Francis was officially certified as a train engineer. Agnes came with him at the station that morning as Mr George handed Francis his certificate and other documentation. The two had not met in all the months Francis had worked at Elephant & Castle though it had felt as if they knew each other. The three had a mini celebration over tea and cake whilst the conversation was peppered with compliments in all directions. Mr George even extended an invitation to Francis and Agnes to join him and his family for a full celebration, which they gladly accepted.

Francis remembered that day as one of the few best days he had experienced in this new country.

12

It was now just about a year and a half since the couple had started working. One morning, whilst working her normal cleaning shift at Heathrow, Agnes felt a severe pain in her stomach. She'd had some discomfort for a few days but had dismissed it. However, the pain she felt that day was far more intense, and clutching her stomach, she crumbled to the restroom floor with her body feeling as if it was on fire. By the time she crawled out into the corridor, she was practically wailing from the biting pain.

As soon as some of the other staff spotted her, they swarmed around her, and in no time, Agnes was rushed to the hospital. It was there that Agnes discovered that she was having a miscarriage. Her heart broke, and she started to wail again. The doctor on duty tried to calm her down, but in the end he had to give up as his patient was inconsolable. Agnes was allowed time to settle before being discharged. Sadly, she had to make her own way home.

That evening when Francis returned home from his shift at the station, Agnes broke the bitter news to him. He was devastated, and he too wept like a baby. He'd been waiting for so long to have his own child, and what should have been a joyful moment, especially as it was a surprise, was pure agony. As soon as he had gathered his emotions, he decided that Agnes should stop working as soon as he got a job as a train engineer. After all, he was already earning a lot more now than he had at Heathrow, so they didn't necessarily need her income. He berated himself for not realising that she needed to slow down; instead, he'd let her become a workaholic like him, allowing circumstances to persuade him that it was acceptable to abandon his traditions and subscribe to the foreigner's belief that a woman could work and earn as much as a man. His mother would be ashamed of what had become of him, and he suddenly felt like a terrible husband.

Agnes, on the other hand felt that she was to blame. As far as she was concerned, she should've known that she was pregnant. It was her body after all, and on top of that, no one wanted to have a child more than her.

"It was your first, Aggie. You couldn't have known," Francis tried to reassure her.

"What if it wasn't?" she replied. "I've felt pain in my stomach before, but I always dismissed it as nothing."

The suggestion that she might have miscarried without knowing deepened Francis' pain. He'd thought that he and Agnes were a perfect match, yet clearly, he couldn't even take care of her. Without him realising, his busy work schedule had taken its toll on his marriage. He'd been too preoccupied with making money and too tired to communicate with his wife these past few months, and it had taken the loss of their unborn baby for him to recognise the error of his ways.

"I should quit," he said.

He couldn't let his work come between him and the bond he shared with Agnes. On top of that, it had taken her so long to conceive, and so the question was how long would it take to happen again, if it ever did.

Agnes did not tolerate his self-loathing and insisted that he keep his job at the station. They had come so far that it would be incredibly foolish to lose everything now when there was still so much at stake. She wasn't going to discard their dreams of owning a house and a car simply because of a miscarriage.

"I'll be fine, Kojo, as long as we have each other," she said.

Her reassurance did nothing to put Francis at ease. In the end, he managed to convince her to take sick leave so that she could recuperate properly.

* * *

During Agnes's time off, a friend she'd made at Afriyie's welcome party informed her that in the UK, people who didn't have a job were entitled to claim benefits. Seeing this as a great opportunity to earn money without working, Agnes immediately applied. After a short time, she started receiving the monthly payments, which helped her pay the bills, and even save a little.

A couple of weeks later, whilst at the station, Francis received an invitation letter to become a train engineer.

No interview. Nothing. He knew Mr George was behind it, so the day after he received that letter, he took two bottles of wine to work for his boss to properly thank him for all he had done. Mr George, though grateful, insisted that it had nothing to do with him. As far as he was concerned, Francis had done it by himself; all he had done was open a door for a man who was already capable of the job.

Later that evening, when Francis told Agnes about his new job, she was so thrilled — in fact, jubilant. It made him feel like he'd just become a president. Adwoa also shared in their joy, praising Francis for his hard work, and encouraging him to reach for greater heights. Shen then insisted that they throw a small family party to celebrate.

Francis was confused by Adwoa' actions. He'd thought she hated him because ever since he'd started climbing up the job ladder, she'd basically avoided him and bluntly refused to even speak to him. This was in contrast to her behaviour when he'd first arrived in the UK, when she had treated him as if she loved him dearly. It was in part her unpredictable behaviour that had pushed him to strive for more. And now that he could finally boast of a decent job with decent pay, he was itching to leave her flat.

Adwoa made a few delicacies for the party all by herself, though Agnes and Francis both contributed. The celebration was indeed small as Afriyie couldn't make it to the party — she was on duty. However, she called to wish her brother-in-law well, which meant so much more to Francis than all the food Adwoa had cooked, because he didn't trust her as far as he could throw her.

*   *   *

The next few months went by incredibly fast. Francis was making enough money from his driving shifts, supplemented by a few cleaning shifts, for him to insist that Agnes quit her job. He bought groceries for their home and paid off a few pending bills just to show his sincere gratitude to Adwoa for housing and feeding them.

However, he soon started to notice that his payslips had been tampered with and his letters half-opened. At first, he thought he might have imagined it until the next payslip came and confirmed his fear. The thought of his employer trying to reduce his pay came to his mind. After all, he was just an African man in a white man's land, and he didn't expect to be treated fairly. One of his colleagues who worked a shift before him was an African man, too, so Francis jokingly asked him about his payments. The man laughed heartily and even went so far as to praise the company for its timely and complete payslips. With that, Francis realised there and then that his enemy was closer to home than he'd thought.

Though he couldn't quite believe it and hated himself for even considering it, Agnes was the only person he could think of to confront since he knew that she was usually at home when his payslips arrived.

"I can't believe this!" she exclaimed. "How can you accuse me of tampering with your letters?"

She paced the room, folding and unfolding her arms. Francis could practically see the smoke of anger rising from the top of her head. Meanwhile, Agnes kept asking herself over and over again how her beloved husband could accuse her of something she would never do. She couldn't imagine invading his privacy regardless of the fact that they were married; what made matters worse was the way in which his accusing eyes hurt and stripped her bare. The judgement on his face was too much for her to bear, so she grabbed a pillow and cried into it.

"Calm down, please," Francis implored her.

Agnes ignored him and ran out of the room, sobbing softly. Francis remained behind, sitting on the bed and resisting the urge to follow her. If it wasn't Agnes, then who else would be so bold as to invade his privacy so recklessly? He couldn't think of anyone else close enough, and so Agnes was, unfortunately, top of the list. However, when he thought about it long and hard, he came to the conclusion that there was absolutely no reason for his wife to do that. Why? Well, for one, he told Agnes everything, even down to what he got paid from each of his jobs and what he spent outside of the bills. He also gave her some money every day before he left for work because although he knew that she'd never spend it, he derived a sense of satisfaction knowing that he could provide for her in this way.

When he broached the subject again a few days later, Agnes resolutely declared her innocence yet again, and they had another argument. Francis knew that he could trust her, but he didn't know how to go about catching the real culprit. He wanted to find out who was checking his payslips before the person graduated to taking his money.

A couple of days later, the truth unexpectedly came to light. While Agnes was lounging on the couch in the living room, Asantewaa came to her. Adwoa had dropped her off after school before returning to work. Agnes took Asantewaa into her arms and ran a hand down her back. She missed the times she'd spent with the little girl back in Ghana, when it had been just the two of them. Agnes had revelled in pampering and caring for her. With Adwoa in the picture, things were different. She was strict with Asantewaa and unforgiving, and whenever Agnes tried to intervene, Adwoa would coldly remind her that Asantewaa wasn't her child.

These reminders always made Agnes feel small, but they didn't stop her from showering Asantewaa with affection whenever she could. In fact, the distance Adwoa tried to create between them only served to make Agnes love Asantewaa more. However, the joy she expected to see on the girl's face was missing here in London, and in its place had appeared anxiety that a child should not have to bear.

Agnes now took a proper look at Asantewaa, at the faint femininity that was sprouting in the 13-year-old girl. She could recall a time when Asantewaa had been just a toddler and completely dependent on her. Agnes was glad to witness such immense growth, knowing that she had almost single-handedly made it happen.

"What's wrong, Asantewaa?" she asked.

"I saw Mum take Daddy's letters and open them," Asantewaa replied.

"Are you sure, Asantewaa?" Agnes asked. "She must have been bringing in the letters."

Asantewaa shook her head vigorously. Agnes shook her head too. She didn't believe Asantewaa. Francis contributed to the housekeeping already, so she couldn't think of any reason why Adwoa would do something like that.

Refusing to believe Asantewaa, Agnes kept the information to herself. However, Asantewaa kept repeating the same thing for days afterwards. Consequently, Agnes decided to confide in the only person that mattered in this situation and who could make sense of it all. Francis was flabbergasted to hear that Adwoa was the culprit. He couldn't understand why she felt she had to go down that path, especially considering that she hadn't helped him in any way to get a job. He was certain she just wanted to make sure that he was contributing enough to the household based on his income, but it made no sense for her to go about it in the way she had. In fact, nothing made sense to him anymore. Suddenly, living in Adwoa's flat no longer felt comfortable, or safe for that matter.

Agnes suggested confronting her sister, and at first, Francis agreed. Then, after taking a step back, he changed his mind.

"It's too risky to fight her because she could decide to kick us out of the house, and then we'll have nowhere to go," he said.

No matter how upset Francis was about Adwoa' actions, he and Agnes definitely needed a roof over their heads because getting a place of their own was very expensive. He was by no means ready for it yet; he needed to save up more money first.

"I'll get another job so we can get out of her hair as soon as possible," Agnes said.

And this time, Francis didn't object.

So, they doubled their hustle, between them working day and night shifts, while keeping their knowledge about Adwoa's despicable behaviour quiet. At the same time, to avoid her, Agnes spent more time at Afriyie's place. It became her safe haven, a place where she could unwind and escape the animosity she felt towards her other sister.

One afternoon while Agnes was with her, Afriyie received an unexpected phone call. On the other end of the line was a woman who Agnes heard say something unbelievable.

"I just saw your youngest sister, and she was speaking badly of you. She was gossiping and spreading details about your infertility."

Obviously, this was a deeply sensitive subject for Afriyie, which was tied to a traumatic fall she'd suffered years ago while pregnant. So, she immediately went on the defensive.

"Agnes would never say such a thing!" she told the caller. Then she handed the phone to her, so she could address the accusation directly.

"Why are you telling lies?" Agnes demanded to know, shocked and upset.

Before any real explanation could be given, the caller abruptly hung up. The sisters were left bewildered by the incident, unaware that this moment would mark the beginning of a slow and painful unravelling of their once-close relationship.

13

A few months later, disaster struck again. It was late at night, and Francis was about to fall asleep when Agnes suddenly screamed. He could hear the pain in her voice even before he saw her wriggling on the bed, and he immediately sat up and took her in his arms. But as his eyes fell on the bedsheet, he screamed too — the sheets were covered in blood.

"Not again!" he called out, tears in his eyes.

They had lost another baby. Agnes had told him a few weeks earlier that she was pregnant. She already had a small bump that was only visible when she wasn't dressed. He'd warned her to be extra careful with work, and she'd gone down to a single shift per day to be on the safe side. Having done all that, they had both been hopeful that this was to be the year that they would have their first child. He thought of his mother who had 12 children, as did Agnes's mum, so they both came from highly fertile families. At one point he'd given in and admitted to Agnes that he felt that they were not destined to have their own children. Agnes had been highly offended by this since she desperately wanted to give birth to her own child and to experience motherhood to the fullest.

So, to him, it therefore made no sense that she'd still miscarried. He felt like the universe was against them. As Agnes sobbed quietly, tears streamed down his cheeks. He held on to her and ran his fingers through her hair. Any words of consolation just stuck in his throat.

While they quietly nursed their pain, the door opened and Adwoa walked in. She looked sleepy, but the moment her eyes zeroed in on the bed, they filled with sympathy. She immediately hugged Agnes to console her.

"I'll take time off work to take you to a specialist," she promised.

However, Francis didn't wait around for Adwoa to clear her work schedule, and the following day, he took Agnes to the hospital himself.

* * *

The doctor, a kind black man, sympathised with them. He explained that miscarriages were quite common and not always a sign of underlying issues.

"A lot of women go through a few miscarriages before having their babies," he said. "I know it's painful, but I want you to know that you aren't alone and you're a healthy, strong woman."

He instructed Agnes to take things easy and recommended some foods and fruits to boost her immune system. The encouragement from the doctor revived her hopes.

However, the loss of their second baby pushed Francis to the edge, and as a result, he worked even harder. He took on additional jobs and only returned home when he felt close to dropping dead. Agnes became worried, yet Francis claimed he was fine and reminded her that as a soldier, he was used to an even harsher lifestyle.

"But you're no longer a soldier, Kojo," she pointed out. "This is London."

Francis shrugged and laughed. He didn't heed her concerns and continued to work tirelessly in order to earn as much money as he could. His plan was simple; he wanted to leave Adwoa' house fast. He couldn't trust her anymore.

When Agnes realised that there was no stopping her husband, she also went back to work. She started with another cleaning agency, one of the biggest in London, which focused only on private homes. Agnes took on five family homes and worked five days a week. The pay was great, and she also got to bond with each of the families. They also welcomed her into their homes, and the easy relationships she had with them meant she didn't feel so lonely when Francis was away at work. At the weekend, when she was home, she would help Adwoa cook and clean. However, Adwoa, instead of complimenting Agnes'ss work ethic, warned her against working too much and losing another pregnancy.

Agnes was inclined to believe that her sister's words came from a place of love and concern for her well-being. Yet she also couldn't forget how Adwoa hadn't wanted her and Francis to work in the first place. For reasons unknown, she wanted them to remain completely dependent on her and have nothing to show for their stay in London. It was her persistent infringement on Francis's privacy that really got to Agnes though, and because she couldn't confront her, the anger festered, so that she began to resent her sister. She could never see her sister in the same way again. Her trust in her was completely shattered. That said, Agnes didn't hate Adwoa; she would just rather avoid her. Given how hard Francis worked, it was clear that their stay with her sister would come to an end soon enough, and that expectation gave Agnes enough reason to tolerate Adwoa.

A few weeks after the miscarriage, Asantewaa came and reported Adwoa's deeds to Agnes again. Now, she knew she had to do something to prevent the situation from getting out of control.

"Stop telling me," she said good-naturedly to Asantewaa. "Just be a good child to your mother."

Agnes feared Asantewaa might one day confront her mother about it, and she didn't want that to happen. She wanted to make sure everything remained smooth so that she and Francis could leave Adwoa's house peacefully.

* * *

Finally, in the middle of 1989, things took a turn for the better when Francis returned home from his evening driving shift.

"I think we have enough money to buy our own house," he announced out of the blue.

At first, Agnes didn't believe him until he pulled out all his payslips from a small wooden box where he'd locked them away. That night, she and Francis did a lot of calculating and soon came to the conclusion that they not only had enough money, but they even had some to spare once Agnes's payslips were added. Deciding that it would be best to keep their plans a secret from Adwoa as well as Afriyie, Francis started house hunting. With the help of a colleague at the station, he was able to get in contact with an estate agent. The agent's fee was decent enough for Francis, so he hired the man — a Mr Bakshi.

Francis couldn't believe how difficult it was to find a suitable home. He spent weeks going from property to property with Mr Bakshi, yet not once did he see a thing he liked. Agnes had described her taste to him, and he was yet to find a place in that style anywhere. Since they were keeping everything hush-hush, she couldn't go with him. However, at the very last moment, when he'd almost lost all hope, Francis finally found what he wanted.

Securing the mortgage proved to be a problem however, as he realised that he couldn't use his real name on the deeds since he as Francis Oppong, didn't have the legal right of stay in the UK. Francis was sufficiently concerned about the situation to discuss it with Mr Bakshi.

"That's very common," Mr Bakshi laughed off his concerns. "Don't worry. As soon as you get your resident's permit and all the other documents to certify that you're eligible to remain in the UK, you'll be able to change your name, not only on your identity card but also on the deeds for the house."

Francis wasn't even sure when he'd finally get his resident's permit. He then got cold feet when he imagined Agnes's brother laying claim to his property and not being able to defend himself given that he wasn't the real Charles Nimako.

"Charles is different from Adwoa," Agnes assured him. "I trust him with my life. He'd never do anything to hurt me."

After much deliberation, Francis's fears were allayed, and Agnes went along with him. Using their fake identities, their new home was signed over to them. Francis could never have imagined that a single document could hold so much weight and importance. As he held on to the contract on their way back to Adwoa's home, he felt whole again. The contract was the answer to all his problems.

Francis and Agnes did not move out straightaway though; there were still a few things he needed to put in place before they could break the news to Adwoa. It took a few months, but when he was finally ready, Francis told Agnes to set up a meeting with both of her sisters.

Agnes therefore called Afriyie and invited her over. It was a Sunday, so Adwoa was at home. When they were all seated, Francis stood up from the couch where he had been sitting next to Agnes and cleared his throat.

"Thank you both so much for your consistent help since Agnes and I moved here," he told the sisters. "Now, we have some news for you. Agnes and I are moving out."

Adwoa leapt up from her seat. "What do you mean you're moving out?" she exclaimed. "I've treated you like a brother. Why did you keep this from me?"

Francis laughed, but he resisted the powerful urge to bring up her invasion of his privacy. He knew he'd gain nothing from it, and after all, he was leaving her house.

"I'm grateful for everything you've done for us, Sister Adwoa," he replied respectfully.

As Afriyie watched and waited for him to continue, he then pulled out the house documents and handed them to her. Her approval was all that mattered to him. After she scanned through the documents, a big smile appeared on her lips.

"I'm so happy for both of you," she said. "You made it!"

She stood up and pulled Agnes into a tight hug. Reluctantly, even Adwoa, with a face like thunder, joined in the hug. Agnes wept with happiness and relief. She couldn't believe that her struggles were finally over.

Asantewaa stood by the door, and quietly sobbing, she walked into the room. Agnes pulled away from her sisters and knelt before her niece. As she took her into her arms, tears streaked down Agnes's cheeks.

"I'll always come and visit you," she promised the girl.

"I'll miss you," Asantewaa replied sadly.

Later that day in the month of November 1989, Agnes and Francis, with their few bags of clothes, let Afriyie drive them to their new home in Firs Close, Mitcham, and the promise of a better future.

14

Over the following months, Francis and Agnes settled into their new home. It was a tidy one-bedroom flat on the second floor in a new development. Living in their own place was a dream come true. Francis felt that he could finally breathe after what had felt like an eternity. He was done with walking on eggshells and could come and go as he pleased. Most importantly, he would never have to come in and find his letters opened. One of the first things that the couple did soon after moving in was to invite Mr Bakshi for a thank you dinner. As far as Francis was concerned, this was the man who had given them the opportunity to start their new life and had guided them through every step of the process.

Francis revelled in the fact that he was no longer confined to the bedroom whenever Adwoa returned from work. He could set foot anywhere in the flat at any time without worrying about whether or not he'd run into her and her antagonistic attitude. He and Agnes turned the living room into their little haven — somewhere they could eat in peace and openly discuss things every night after work before retiring to the sanctuary of their bedroom.

One evening after dinner, Francis sat beside Agnes on the living-room floor and circled his thumb on the insides of her palms.

"Do you miss Sister Adwoa?" he asked.

"I'm not sure, Kojo," she replied. "But I miss Asantewaa so much. I want to see her every day, but I know I can't."

The first few days after they'd left Adwoa's flat, Agnes had consistently reached out to her sister to speak to Asantewaa on the phone, but her mother always had an excuse as to why Agnes could not speak with her niece. It was either, 'Asantewaa is asleep', or 'Asantewaa is doing some chores'. It became evident with time that Adwoa simply didn't want Agnes to maintain her close relationship with Asantewaa. That hurt Agnes, but she didn't regret leaving Adwoa's home.

"I miss Asantewaa, too," Francis conceded. "But I don't miss that place."

In fact, he felt on top of the world and was at his happiest in those intimate moments with his wife.

After the initial euphoria, it was time to initiate the routine that would allow them to stay on top of their mortgage payments. They had paid the five per cent deposit required to secure the mortgage, but that meant they now had to repay the remaining 95 per cent. That was a lot of money for them, and it meant they had to keep working very hard for a long time to achieve their goal. Yet Francis was up to the task. In fact, he didn't care about the 25 years it would take to finish the payments especially as he was determined to pay it off earlier.

With their goal in mind, he worked even harder. Agnes was also determined to contribute and continued with her cleaning job. Supporting Francis and realising their dream was her focus. It was a lot of work though, and on most days after her shift, she'd return home completely exhausted. Cooking daily meals was an additional chore. So, although it was expensive, once in a while she bought takeouts for dinner.

Francis didn't mind takeouts; he even welcomed the idea because he felt that Agnes was allowed to take a break to unwind. In fact, if he had his way, he wouldn't let her work a day in her life as he understood how gruelling their routine was. For that reason, he often showered her with praise for working so hard, though he also advised her to take things easy.

"I'm the head of the home, Aggie. You don't have to work so hard," he would say. "If it's too much, you can take a few days off."

"It's our home, Kojo, and I appreciate how hard you work, but I want to be able to help as much as possible," she would reply.

"Remember what the doctor said," he reminded her.

The thought of the loss of their babies always came to haunt Francis in moments like these. While Agnes tried to push the sad memories to the back of her mind, the ordeal still felt painful and fresh for both of them; missing Asantewaa doubled the pain. She'd raised Asantewaa as her child, and the girl had filled the emptiness she'd felt back then. Not having her around now meant that on days when Francis was away at work, Agnes would walk around the house, forlorn. It was too big for her and Francis alone, and she longed to hear the cries of a baby ringing through the house, and to run around the large rooms chasing a toddler. She was even looking forward to cleaning up after messy children.

Whenever she was caught up in those thoughts, despite having achieved one of their key goals in life by buying their own home, the future still looked bleak. Agnes knew that having her own child was the only balm for the deep wound in her heart. Yet at the same time, she also understood that carrying a pregnancy to full term was completely out of her hands. After the second miscarriage, she'd decided to leave everything to God. She believed that if God wanted her to have a child, it would happen. However, this faith didn't stop the pain.

* * *

Francis worked weekends, and feeling quite lost one Sunday morning, Agnes decided to visit Adwoa. She took her time to get ready for the 35-minute bus ride because she wanted to arrive nice and relaxed for a pleasant afternoon with her sister and niece. When she arrived, Asantewaa opened the front door. Tears blurred Agnes's vision as she pulled the teenager into a tight hug. She couldn't believe that Asantewaa had grown so much in such a short time.

Adwoa had a visitor whom Agnes had never seen before, but because of their tense relationship, she couldn't bring herself to ask her sister who it was. The man seemed to be the same age as Adwoa, and he was rather handsome too. They were sitting next to each other on the couch, holding hands, but pulled apart when Agnes walked in.

"This is Mr Kusi." Adwoa introduced the man to Agnes but didn't elaborate on exactly who he was.

"It's a pleasure to finally meet you," Mr Kusi remarked in a friendly voice. "Adwoa has told me so much about you."

Agnes simply nodded and sat down on the couch, keeping Asantewaa close beside her. She wanted to believe that Adwoa had said good things about her to Mr Kusi, but she knew that her sister was still offended because she and Francis hadn't let her in on their plans to buy a house. A few minutes after Agnes had arrived, Mr Kusi became uncomfortable and excused himself. Adwoa didn't seem elated by Agnes's visit either.

"You could have called before coming," she told her.

"You don't always pick up the phone, Sister Adwoa. Besides, I wanted to see Asantewaa. It's been so long, and she's grown so big."

"Only in your eyes," Adwoa said haughtily. "She looks the same to me."

Agnes pulled Asantewaa closer and ruffled her braids. "I think I'm allowed to visit Asantewaa, regardless."

"It's not like I can stop you from doing anything," Adwoa countered.

The atmosphere in the room immediately changed from heated to flaming hot. Agnes wanted to leave immediately, but she decided otherwise because of Asantewaa. Asantewaa was still impressionable, and she didn't want her to think that her aunt didn't want to see her anymore.

When Adwoa had stopped taking her calls, Agnes had voiced her concerns to Afriyie. Afriyie had laughed at Agnes's worries and insisted that Adwoa would eventually come to terms with their sudden departure. However, it had been six months now, and Adwoa continued to hold the grudge close to her heart. In addition, whenever Agnes brought up the matter with Afriyie, the latter remained impartial because she didn't want to get involved in the problems between her sisters. She would always end the conversation by saying that Agnes and Adwoa should find a way to bury the hatchet.

After several moments of silence, Adwoa stood up.

"I'll be in my room," she said and left.

Tears burned Agnes's eyes as she watched her sister march angrily out of the room. She'd thought that seeing Asantewaa again was more important than Adwoa' approval. But she was wrong.

* * *

That night back at home, as she told Francis about her visit, Agnes couldn't stop the tears from streaming down her cheeks. She couldn't understand why her sister despised her so much. All her life, she'd loved and cherished her older siblings, praying for their success and progress because she knew that this would also determine how her own future would turn out. The invitation to the UK had proved as much since it had been the beginning of the answers to Agnes's prayers. It had felt that way then, but now, Agnes was no longer sure that she'd made the right decision in coming to London.

"It's fine, Aggie," Francis consoled her. "I'm sure she'll come around eventually."

He, on the other hand, had realised a long time ago that Adwoa didn't want his progress. It had been apparent from the moment she had discouraged them from working. She was clearly jealous of everything he'd managed to achieve, but he couldn't understand why she also begrudged her own sister, and for so long at that. It was a situation that did not make sense to him. However, Francis couldn't bring himself to point out Adwoa's faults to Agnes.

Agnes also briefly mentioned Mr Kusi to Francis, and since she was curious about him, she eventually called Afriyie and learnt that he was Adwoa's boyfriend. Agnes wondered how Asantewaa was handling it all and whether she was comfortable with a stranger in her home. Her heart went out to the little girl.

It was the last time that Agnes would see Adwoa and her Asantewaa for a very long time.

* * *

About six months or so after moving into the flat, a situation that Agnes had completely forgotten about came back to haunt her. It was one of those rare Sundays when Francis was home early from his shift. Agnes was lying on the sofa with her head in his lap when they heard a knock on the front door. They never had surprise visitors — even the neighbours phoned before coming over — so Agnes was surprised. She jumped up from the sofa and went to the door. When she opened it, she froze. Outside were two police officers who flashed their warrant cards to confirm their identity.

"We'd like to speak with Agnes Nimako," they said.

Agnes was shaking. Meanwhile, Francis appeared behind her and put his arms around her.

"What do you want?" he asked the mean-looking police officers.

Agnes thought there had to be a mistake and tried to explain that whatever it was, she was innocent. But when the police officers explained their reason for barging in on them, she lost her voice.

After having received unemployment benefit while out of work after her miscarriage some two years before, she had been expected to cancel it as soon as she got a new job. However, she had failed to do so.

Francis turned a frustrated gaze towards Agnes. Throughout his time in the UK, his motto had always been, 'Never get involved with the police'. All the warnings Adwoa had drummed into him had stuck like glue. They were not legal residents, and they had used false identities to get jobs. Just one of these misdemeanours was enough to get them arrested and even deported. He knew that

Agnes was also aware of this, so he was truly baffled to learn about what she had done ... or not done.

"You are both expected to remain in the country while we carry out our investigation," the police officers told them before leaving.

A few days later, a letter arrived informing Agnes and Francis that they both had to appear at the local magistrates' court for a hearing.

* * *

Agnes didn't have any excuse for her actions. As she sat glumly on the wooden bench in the court, she realised that she wasn't even remorseful, because in truth, she'd known all along that there would be repercussions in the long run. In fact, she'd been waiting for the day.

After resuming work at the end of her sick leave, she knew that the right thing to do was to stop claiming the benefits, but she had become comfortable with and dependent on the extra money. For a while, she vacillated and expected that eventually she would put a stop to them — until she realised that she simply didn't want to. The extra funds had made such a big difference to the household income. Combined with her payslips from her shifts, it was a significant amount. Eventually, the love of money became stronger than the desire to do the right thing, to the point that she even convinced herself that she was not breaking the law. In any event, she had rationalised; the world hadn't been fair to her and her husband anyway, what with the way they worked so hard and struggled for every penny. Having their own home hadn't made things any easier, really. The mortgage loan they had to pay back was huge, and the bills were many. On top of that were other extra but obligatory expenses that all immigrants had. They both sent money back home to their families, and she had started building a house complete with 14 bedrooms for her family back in Sunyani. Agnes also knew that she couldn't leave everything to Francis. The flat was their home, not just his, and she wanted to contribute to their success, which is why she needed all the money she could get. After all that reasoning, the decision was made — she would not cancel the benefits, and she did not tell Francis because she knew that he wouldn't have approved.

Even as Agnes was interrogated, and harshly at that, she still felt sad about having to say goodbye to the extra money and what it meant for their finances. Fortunately, despite being found guilty of benefit fraud, she escaped a prison sentence but was asked to pay a hefty fine. In contrast with Agnes's laissez-faire attitude, Francis had a very different view, and when they got home that night, he berated Agnes for her nonchalance.

"What were you thinking?" he shouted. "You know how the UK frowns on illegal immigrants. Why would you deliberately put us in front of the law?"

"I'm sorry, Kojo," she replied. "The extra money came in handy. I didn't think to consider the consequences."

Francis hated being at the mercy of others. For a while after settling into their new home, he'd basked in the peace that came with being in control of his life, but the gruelling session at the court had disturbed that peace. He really wanted to have a good go at his wife, but he couldn't, because he knew that she'd done everything with good intentions. He also secretly felt guilty for what had happened and blamed himself for Agnes's behaviour because it meant that he wasn't doing enough as a man. The bottom line was that he should have had enough money to give Agnes everything she could ever wish for. Then she wouldn't have to work so hard, nor would she have to take money from the government. For the first time in a long time, he felt ashamed of the husband he was.

Meanwhile, the court hearing had opened his eyes to the realities of the British system. The case had been termed minor, yet he'd been made to feel like he and Agnes had committed a heinous crime. In any case, he knew that proceedings would be recorded into the system, and that realisation really disturbed him. He didn't want their false identities to attract unwanted attention, fearing that if that happened, they would have to pay an even higher price.

* * *

Agnes returned to work, but there was something different about her. As Francis' words continued to ring in her ears, she became solemn and extremely cautious. For example, whenever she shopped for groceries and felt that she was being cheated at the counter, she resisted the urge to question anything so as not to draw attention to herself. She was determined not to end up on the wrong side of the law again because there was no guarantee that she would not be handed a harsher punishment. In addition, the racism and the way she had been patronised was unbearable; everyone in the court had treated her like a dimwit. They'd made a blatant show of correcting and 'educating' her at the slightest opportunity despite the fact that Agnes could read and write better than many Londoners. The judgment she'd been subjected to had made her feel inferior, diminishing her self-esteem. There was no way she was going to put herself through that again.

It didn't just stop there in the court and with white Londoners. A couple of black friends she had made in their neighbourhood stopped visiting. At first, Agnes thought they were busy, so she decided to pay them a visit. Even when she could hear their children running around inside the house, each did not answer her knocks. Agnes realised what had happened; they must have seen the police at their door and put two and two together. One's existence in London life was judged by association, and most people just didn't want to get into trouble, and few would help anyone, especially a foreigner in trouble. Although the sentiment was understandable, their attitude still hurt Agnes, who felt that she was being rejected because they considered her inferior.

"This is how the UK functions, Aggie," Francis sighed. "People are scared of the authorities and the law, and they don't want to be seen with us because they don't want to be implicated in anything that jeopardises their comfy lives."

Francis's argument didn't make Agnes feel any better. Rather, it opened her eyes to the kind of life they were subjected to and the reality that their kids would probably have to face. Suddenly, she wasn't so sure if she really wanted to raise a child in the midst of all this chaos. Sure, Ghana had its problems, but she would never be referred to as an illegal alien in her own home. The thought of her children growing up to face constant discrimination from their peers and the country at large didn't sit well with her. As these thoughts churned round and round in Agnes's mind, she started to hate London. Despite all they'd struggled to achieve, nothing was worth being treated as an outcast. She hated the judgmental stares she got from the neighbours when she got on the bus; the fact that she had to bury her emotional pain and appear strong whenever she faced any form of disrespect; that she had to tolerate everyone else's bad behaviour when no one cared about how she felt; that Francis had to work so hard for so many hours just to get by; and that she had to work so hard to support him. She got to the stage where she hated everything about London. The place was definitely not what she had expected it to be when she was back in Ghana, and she was now at the stage where she would do anything just to go back there to be with her mother.

15

It was now 1991, about a year following Agnes's brush with the law. The couple had managed to re-establish their routine. Then in February 1991, for several days, Agnes experienced unexpected and persistent dizziness. Scared that she might faint during one of her shifts, she booked an appointment with her GP.

* * *

Sitting in the waiting room, whitewashed walls plastered with multiple public health notices, she wondered what could be wrong with her. At the same time, she worried about how much pay she'd lose if she had to take a few days off. She prayed hard that it would not be the case, especially as it would cost her more as prescriptions were so expensive. After her last miscarriage, the doctor had advised her against taking any medicines that were not prescribed, for fear of causing harm to her unborn baby should she become pregnant again.

When one of the nurses eventually called her in, Agnes felt an uneasiness settle in the pit of her stomach.

She desperately wanted to believe that she could be pregnant, but besides feeling dizzy, which could have been attributed to stress from work, she hadn't seen any noticeable changes in her body.

"Congratulations, ma'am. The test results show that you are pregnant," the doctor beamed.

Agnes nodded absent-mindedly, not sure whether she'd heard right. She shook her head and asked to see the test results because she could only be sure when she read the words herself. She'd never had the opportunity to hold a pregnancy-test result in her own hands before because she'd always lost the baby before finding out that she was pregnant.

"Thank you, doctor," she stammered, as she stared at test stick.

She just about managed to say goodbye to the doctor before she left the surgery for the short back home.

* * *

Agnes had no memory of getting home after her appointment. Feeling very restless, she spent the next few hours pacing the entire flat as she waited for Francis to return from work. It was not until Francis finally arrived that her joy finally bubbled over.

"Francis. I'm pregnant," she blurted out before he even had a chance to close the door. He scanned her face and as what she said sunk in, he threw his bag on the floor, grabbed her by the waist and twirled her around.

"We did it!" he exclaimed.

His eyes grew misty as the news sank in. Then all he wanted to do was climb the tallest roof and scream for joy. He danced around the living room with Agnes, then sat on the floor, cradling her in his arms and weeping. Then the worry about what could go wrong crept in.

"You know you have to take it extra easy now, Aggie," he said.

"I know," she replied.

"In fact, I suggest that you take several days off to rest," he added.

Not convinced that Agnes would listen to him, he took it upon himself to take care of her. He woke up very early every day to clean the house and cook. He also took over the grocery shopping so that Agnes would not have to carry anything heavy. The pregnancy was still in its early stages, and he didn't want to take any chances. Agnes was under strict instructions not to lift a finger.

"I promised to take care of you until the baby arrives," he said.

And every day, he was as good as his word.

* * *

The bond between husband and wife became even stronger. Agnes was grateful for Francis. However, Francis himself realised that he was more scared than happy. While at work, he was constantly worried about what Agnes was doing, and his thoughts became so jumbled that he started making mistakes at work. His colleagues complained about his absent-mindedness, and twice, he received a stern warning from one of his bosses. Then the constant pressure meant he picked up a virus and was forced to take a few days off.

While recuperating, Francis realised that in a bid to keep his pregnant wife happy, he was causing more harm than good. He was going about things in the wrong way. Now that he was unwell, Agnes had to take care of him, staying up late to wipe his burning, feverish skin with a wet napkin. He hated himself for allowing his fear of losing the baby to cloud his good judgment and burden the one person he was trying to protect. The truth was that he'd also mourned the miscarriages, and now he had no idea of how to handle the process of waiting for their bundle of joy to arrive. Meanwhile, Agnes fully understood that Francis was scared, so she didn't mind looking after him at all.

* * *

When she was three months pregnant, in May 1991, Francis decided to embrace the happiness and threw a house party for Agnes; it was a small gathering, in fact, so small that the only guests were the two of them. He had briefly thought about inviting a few friends, but he knew that there was a high probability that they wouldn't honour his invitation. They had continued to keep their distance, and he knew that he'd be incredibly hurt if someone he considered a friend or held in high regard turned down his invitation or accepted it and then not showed up. So, he'd decided that a party for two would have to be good enough.

The day dawned brightly. Francis made a few dishes that he was sure Agnes's pregnant palate would tolerate. He had a music tape that he'd bought a long time ago, back when they'd still been in Adwoa's house, that he played using their cassette player. He and Agnes then danced over a candle-lit dinner dressed in their best party clothes. Francis wore a tailored dark suit, while Agnes wore her favourite maternity dress with a beautiful floral hem. Francis loved that his wife was so happy, radiating more than the sun itself. Tears stung his eyes as he pulled her into the living room, which he had decorated with balloons. He felt like his heart was about to burst from the excitement of the moment and because of what the future held for them. He twirled her around the room, holding her waist, with both of them laughing non-stop. The romantic music played on even as they stumbled on each other's feet, trying to keep their amusement in check. Francis was the happiest he'd been for a long time, and was sure that whatever happened, he would die a happy man.

"Do you think it'll be a boy or a girl?" Agnes asked.

"I don't care and haven't even thought about it," he replied exuberantly. "I think we should just be grateful to have been given another opportunity to have a baby. Plus, every child is worthy of love and affection regardless of their gender."

His attitude was very different from that of most African men, as they usually wanted a son. Francis just wanted to hold his baby in his arms.

A few days after the party for two, Agnes returned to working a few shifts a week to prepare for the bright future ahead of them, it still took Francis a lot of effort to keep any negative thoughts at bay and fully enjoy the process of waiting for the baby to arrive. Yet any worries he may have had paled into insignificance compared to the upheaval that was to be unleashed on them.

* * *

One evening in early October 1991, when Agnes was eight months pregnant, Francis was resting at home when he heard knocking on the door. In fact, it wasn't knocking but sudden, loud, thunderous banging. *Boom! Boom! Boom!* Francis sat bolt upright, and he was sure his heart had jumped out of his chest. He turned to Agnes who sat frozen next to him then got up to see what the commotion was about.

Before he could reach the door, it flung open with force, making him fall backwards into the hallway. Three uniformed officers stormed in.

"It's the police!" one of them shouted. "We're looking for Francis Oppong!"

He barely had time to process what was happening. "I'm ... I'm Francis. What's this about?"

Without explanation, they told him he was under arrest, something about dishonesty and obtaining property by deception. The words were quick, clinical, confusing. Agnes, terrified and sobbing, tried to speak up, but the officers ignored her.

Francis raised his hands. "Wait … can we talk about this?"

Before he knew it, the officers had slammed him to the ground. Pain shot through his arm as he heard something crack. Winded, stunned and in handcuffs, he turned to Agnes who was screaming his name. She wasn't spared. Despite her being obviously heavily pregnant, she was manhandled as they placed cuffs on her wrists. She begged them to be careful, but they didn't care and was dragged away in tears.

The police dragged them both to Kensington Police Station, where they were separated. He was subjected to a gruelling interrogation. Francis wanted to answer their questions, but he was too stunned, weak and disoriented to speak coherently. What he did pick up during the ordeal was that **their estate agent, Mr Bakshi, had also been arrested.**

*   *   *

The couple remained in separate cells in Kensington for several days before being dragged for a brief court hearing at Horseferry Road Magistrates Court. After that, he was taken to Wormwood Scrubs, whilst Agnes was sent to Holloway Prison. Both were held in the remand wing of their respective prisons; the steel doors slammed behind them. It was the first time in five years that they had been apart, and they had no idea how long it would last.

For the first time since he'd arrived in London, Francis understood his mother's fears and realised how every single one of them had gradually come true. The Blacks didn't have a say in the UK. They were seen and treated like dogs. Francis felt even more terrible because Agnes was made to suffer as well. He'd promised to take care of her, but the police had stripped him of everything that made him a man and rendered him powerless.

* * *

They were both assigned lawyers. At first, Francis was reluctant to speak to his because he now trusted no one. However, because Mr Ben, as he was called, and a fellow Ghanaian sounded experienced and knowledgeable, he slowly let his guard down. In addition, he had appeared to be efficient having gathered what seemed to be the relevant information and paperwork quite quickly. In any event, Francis had no choice but to cooperate with someone if he was to be released and reunited with Agnes.

As they sat in the interrogation room one morning, Francis studied Mr Ben. He did indeed reek of confidence and authority. Francis felt that he was a man who understood the job.

"I promise you I'll make you walk out of prison with your head held high," Mr Ben boasted.

Francis believed him; he just wasn't sure when that would happen. He knew that the police weren't idle, and that they were doing everything to keep him locked up until it was time to go to trial, however long that would take. He also knew that they did not care that he had a wife who was about to give birth. So, Francis had to believe that Mr Ben would get him out.

"I don't want to spend the best part of my life locked up, Mr Ben," he said. "I hope I can trust you."

Mr Ben reassured him and continued with his questioning. Francis answered every question truthfully. Then lawyer stuck his pen behind his ear and asked one critical question.

"Do you have any idea who may have reported you?"

This was the question that Francis slept on and woke up with. He'd spent sleepless nights trying to figure out who might despise him so much as to bring this type of chaos and misery into his life. Yet each time, he'd turned up blank.

"I can't think of anybody."

Mr Ben adjusted his rimless glasses and nodded slowly as he leafed through a bunch of papers on the table.

"Does the name Leticia Adwoa Badu ring a bell?" he asked.

The name did not only ring a bell but also set off a thousand alarms in Francis' head. In fact, he was so shocked that he held his breath for a few seconds longer than was good for him. He gaped at the lawyer as shock waves cascaded down his spine, and he remained speechless for several minutes. The fact of the matter was that he was too scared to ask further questions because he did not want the answers to confirm his suspicions.

"She's my sister-in-law," he eventually whispered. "My wife's older sister. She helped us come to the UK and then allowed us to stay with her for a couple of years."

Mr Ben's face fell. "How is that possible?" he asked. "She's the same woman who reported you to the police and the Home Office for using false identities. She reported you with the help of Mr and Mrs Amponsen. I believe they're her friends."

Francis remembered the Amponsen couple. They'd been very welcoming during his first week in London, and Mrs Amponsen had spent the next couple of weeks cooking for them, insisting that they needed to familiarise their palates with English food. He knew Adwoa was pretty close to the couple, to the point that they would breeze in and out of her flat like they owned the place. Francis had no doubt that she had sought their help in getting him into trouble; he was only confused by their decision to go along with such a wicked thing. He sat rooted to his chair, his head threatening to explode. In deep despair, he slumped down in his chair, wishing that the ground would open up and swallow him. A dark cloud descended over him as flashbacks to the beatings at the hands of the SIB suddenly appeared; the pain in his right hand from the injury he sustained as a result throbbed; and the headaches he suffered as a result of the trauma threatened to come back. With all this going on in his body, he couldn't think clearly.

"Did you do anything to make her want to spite you like this?" Mr Ben asked. He himself could not believe that a man as gentle as his client could have done anything to deserve such a thing.

Francis had no answer for the lawyer. During the time when she'd been snooping around and opening his private letters and payslips, he'd never confronted her because he'd been grateful for her help and had respected her for that. There'd never been a time when he'd argued with her. What had he ever done to Adwoa except try to succeed in London?

"Perhaps it's out of jealousy?" the lawyer prompted him.

Francis knew that Adwoa was envious. He'd figured out that she didn't exactly want him to progress, but never in his life would he have imagined that she'd go to such lengths to betray and hurt him ... and her own sister. Adwoa had been among the people who'd consoled Agnes when he'd been locked up in prison in Ghana, so she knew of every obstacle he'd overcome to get to the UK.

Mr Ben continued to ramble on, but Francis tuned out. He wondered how he was going to tell Agnes that her sister was responsible for the calamity that had befallen them. He wondered whether she would even believe him.

"I've never hurt Adwoa," Francis finally stuttered through the heavy lump in his throat.

Meanwhile, Mr Ben continued to question Francis about a motive for Adwoa's action, even asking if she really was a relative; he secretly hoped that Francis would say something different.

That night Francis counted the breeze blocks in his prison cell and wished he was granted the grace of dying in his sleep. Yet his wish wasn't granted; he remained alive. On top of that, it transpired that Mr Ben wasn't as good a lawyer as he seemed to be because two weeks passed and Francis was still in jail.

* * *

Francis wrote to his beloved Aggie every day. He wasn't allowed to see her, but he needed her to know he was still there, that he loved her and that he was scared too. He asked about the baby constantly as he imagined the bump growing but without him there to hold or talk to. It was very difficult to keep his spirits up inside the grey, cold and heavy walls of Wormwood Scrubs, and the aches that had taken over his body. However, he tried hard to by imagining himself and Aggie back at home getting ready for the birth.

Three weeks after his arrest, he decided to write to his mother-in-law, Mary, to pray for divine help. He was past caring about anything except their immediate release from prison and so far, nothing had worked. By now, the whole of Tanoso had probably heard about their predicament anyway, and in turn, passed the news on to relatives and friends in surrounding villages. So really, he had nothing to lose by writing to her. As soon as the idea came to mind, he asked the guards for pen and paper and wrote a long letter, addressing Mary affectionately as 'Eno

Mmeraa', the title of respect for a mother-in-law, and one he had not uttered for a very long time. In the letter, he asked her to send drinks and other gifts to the Asoneyeso shrine, and to consult the local spirit medium in exchange for their freedom.

16

Every other day, Agnes read her letters from Francis with a real ache in her heart. Over the three weeks since the arrest, she had steadily lost her source of joy. The current situation was far from anything she'd imagined. In fact, being locked up in a cell in London as a pregnant woman was truly the misery of all miseries, something she'd never wish for her enemy. It was nearly impossible to fathom the amount of hatred someone must have had to put them through such an ordeal.

Agnes strongly believed that the universe was against them. That was the only explanation she could come up with to justify how everything had collapsed on them. The female guards, all white women, looked upon Agnes with genuine concern because of her pregnancy. However, Agnes returned the favour with disdain and hated them for serving a system that was so unjust to the helpless. She felt that the entire UK system was rigged and that the whole country was against the blacks, their sole aim being to reduce them to nothing and rip them of their dignity. In a way, in her case, it had succeeded in doing just that.

They might have rendered her dreams hopeless, but her soul remained intact, and with the letters from Francis encouraging her to hold on and remain strong, Agnes was determined to face every battle head on and see her pregnancy to the end. Her unborn baby became the only reason she had to see a new day. It was the same motivation that made her open her mouth to shove tasteless, watery meals down her throat. It was only because she needed to eat for her baby. She'd struggled through the entire eight months ad she wasn't going to let anything stop her during the final lap.

The days were long and unending. Agnes's nightly ritual became the tears that consistently burned down her hollow cheeks. She missed Francis so much - even the waiting up for him to return from work so they'd have dinner together, and their playful, meaningless banter. In the end, the letters were like a double edged sword that really only served to portray how bad their situation was.

* * *

After he had handed the letter to one of the guards for posting, Francis knew that the rest was left to him. As he considered his next step, he too looked forward to, but also dreaded receiving letters from Agnes. He couldn't tell if she was really coping or if she was pretending to be fine just to put his mind at ease. On the other hand, he wasn't sure whether he'd be able to handle the truth about her struggles either. The letters only served as a reminder of how much he'd failed as a husband and a protector. He'd left her out in the wild to be devoured while all he could do was simply watch without being able to raise a finger. They'd been blessed with their long-awaited baby only for him to mess it up. Everything was his fault. P mlain and simple.

As the head of the home, he should've been able to avert some certain situations, but hadn't; instead he'd not only dragged himself down another pit, he'd also dragged his pregnant wife in with him. A whole family locked up in prison. He was assailed by the guilt of it all and the thought of how everything could've been different if he'd just stayed at Adwoa's. One thing he was sure of was that she would not have ratted them if they were still with her. His singular decision to be a man of his own had rendered him powerless. Every day, he ended his ruminations wishing he could turn back the hands of time to before they had even thought of buying the flat. He would have even given up working if it had meant keeping Agnes free from all this headache. The only thing was that he knew that he wasn't the type of man to eternally depend on someone else. He ran his fingers across the scribbled words of the letter and wondered why things had to be so tough for them. From prisoner to fugitive and prisoner again. He felt like he was in some kind of twisted cycle of suffering. Some people had it easy and why he wasn't one of them was a mystery to him.

He read that day's letter again, very slowly, savouring the very ink of each letter in every word, and how they made his heart pump hard with affection and love. His mind conjured up Agnes standing right before him and saying the words directly to him instead. He imagined it so hard and long that it almost felt real. He blinked away the image, more to keep the painful sting from erupting into full blown tears than to wipe the vision of Agnes from his head.

Francis thought about everything he'd planned for the arrival of his baby including a small surprise baby shower. Plans had already been taking shape but they now lay in tatters because he was locked up, and this time, there was no escaping. Security was heavy and tight. This was definitely not the rickety one-room mess of the guard room at the SIB. Worse, in addition to the heavy steel bars, there no windows. With all this, he resigned himself to a fate unknown. It also appeared that the other prisoners in his wing had done the same; they all seemed to have made peace with their situation too. In some faces, Francis could see hopelessness and nonchalance. They were happy to be served the crappy meals and joked about with the security guards. Some of them slept like logs of wood as if they had not a care in the world. His own cellmate, James, did however lighten the mood with his many untitled, self-penned and tuneless songs that he sang throughout the day.

When Francis realised he was the only one who was overwhelmed by his misery, he too tried to join in on the banter and bad jokes but he couldn't keep up. He knew that as long as Agnes remained in prison, he could never have peace of mind — well not enough to sleep soundly anyway. He didn't mind if he had to stay in prison and she released. As a trained army man, he could handle himself but Agnes was just a helpless woman. Francis couldn't imagine how uncomfortable it must have been for her confined within four walls and sleeping on a thin mattress. Thinking about it broke his heart.

* * *

Two weeks after sending the letter off, Francis took another decisive step and fired Mr Ben. The lawyer who had seemed so competent at first had not delivered on his promise and furthermore, had not bothered to communicate with Francis for a nearly three weeks since his first visit.

The justice system was oddly fair in some respects because within 48 hours, Francis was seen by another lawyer. This one was a Mr Nicolson, a big and burly white man who at the first visit, was able to pick up just where Mr Ben had left off. After their first meeting, he informed he would send word through the officers on progress with the paperwork until their next meeting. Francis though wary to make a quick judgement this time round was somehow reassured. Perhaps Eno Mmeraa's consultation at the shrine had proved to be effective.

As a youngster he'd heard so much about the shrine. Everyone in Tanoso and the surrounding villages spoke of its power. Even his father had at times paid homage at and occasionally it was rumoured that his herbs got their potency from the shrine. For this reason, Francis was quite hopeful that the case would die a natural death with an intervention from Eno Mmeraa. If it did, it would be a miracle. The thought of him walking hand-in-hand with Agnes as they made their way out of the prison doors soothed him. It would surely shock the Londoners even with their own religion and show them what the blacks were made of.

However, Francis' hopefulness lasted for only a short while. His weariness grew when some prisoners in the cell beside his broke into a fight and one of them was stabbed. Before the security could intervene, the unknown guy had died. A cold chill coursed through Francis as he saw blood flowing from the cell into the corridor. The so-called breakfast he'd eaten that morning threatened to spew out. Every prisoner stuck their nose out through the iron bars, trying to catch a glimpse of the dead guy as the prison medical team wheeled him out. The rest of the prisoners who had been involved in the melee followed soon after, handcuffed amid grumbles and protests.

Francis turned wide eyes to James.

"Will they march us out too?"

James chuckled, seemingly unaffected by the recent event replied, "The fight doesn't really concern us. But if they decide to march us out, who are we to argue?"

"But someone died," Francis insisted.

James slapped a hand on Francis' shoulders. "If you stay here long enough, you'll find that there's at least one murder every other week."

Francis shook his head bitterly but didn't say another word. He didn't like the idea of staying 'long enough'. The thought of someone stabbing him to death when he hadn't got Agnes out of jail scared the hell out of him. There were a lot of things at stake, things that James and the others had no clue about. His growing family was his priority. Francis knew that Agnes would never forgive him if he ended up dead … in prison … leaving her to give birth to their much wanted baby alone. For him, knowing that the baby was due at any time with him not being there to hold Agnes's hand as he had promised was just as bad as death itself. In his current position, that promise felt like it had been made a lifetime before, when he thought that everything was perfect and would remain so forever. How naïve of him to have thought so. Now the house he had built was tumbling down, brick by brick, and to make matters worse, the first blow had been struck by family — by Adwoa.

Before he spiralled down into an abyss of despair, Francis forced himself to focus on the outcome he wanted. Using the mental agility he had acquired as a soldier seemingly trapped in the harshest of conditions, he forced himself to think of baby names. That worked momentarily, but he was soon forced to face the fact that he could not keep Agnes in the dark about what he had found out from Mr Ben. So, he wrote a long letter, first professing his undying love for her before breaking the news about Adwoa's involvement in their predicament. As he gave the letter to the prison officer to post for him, he was told that Agnes had been moved to Willington Hospital for a brief medical examination and that they would have to either wait until she was discharged or find another way to get it to her.

The news deflated Francis. He'd been confident in the fact that Agnes and the baby were doing well, but with this new information, his heart hardened in his chest. The officer, seeing Francis's reaction, reassured him that Agnes was just fine and had simply gone for a routine check-up. Francis didn't believe it though. He couldn't bring himself to believe anything that came from the mouth of a policeman and so begged to be allowed to see Agnes for himself. Unsurprisingly, he was bluntly refused, and was reminded that the only way he would leave prison was if his bail was posted.

Francis knew that Agnes was a strong woman but being locked up in a cell would have been a real test for her. Yet again, he blamed himself for failing his wife. For the next few days, he wrote more letters to her, hoping that she would pick them up after she was discharged. After about a week, even though it had been confirmed that Agnes was back in Holloway, he had yet to receive a reply. That was unusual. He pestered the security guards and the officer in charge of the letters, and even though they reassured him that Agnes had received his letters, he refused to believe them. There was no way that the wife he knew would read his letters and ignore them. He then demanded to phone the hospital. The prison officers allowed him to, if only to get him off their backs. When

Francis did get through, the voice on the other end of the line told him that Agnes had indeed been transferred back to Holloway.

Francis became even more apprehensive. He didn't understand why she was being taken in and out of prison and not having answers to his many burning questions made him feel sick. He began to imagine all sorts including whether Agnes was deliberately not answering his letters. Was the realisation that it was her own sister who had effectively had them arrested so heart-wrenching that she couldn't communicate? Confused, Francis wrote another letter, pleading that she make time to talk to him on the phone. Then he waited for her response.

* * *

Before Agnes's response came a few days later, loud sirens blaring roused Francis from a restless sleep. Apparently, a group of prisoners had taken it upon themselves to escape through the kitchen wing. The officers-in-charge banged heavily on the iron bars and demanded that everyone step out. Francis, James and the other prisoners were marched out to an open field where they were forced to engage in some simple drills. It was early morning; the dew was heavy on the ground; the cold was biting, and it most certainly wasn't drill day.

The guards then ordered them to file out in their numbers and according to their cell wings. The C wing, Francis' wing, made up the third row. Francis rubbed a hand across his face and forced back a heavy yawn. He didn't understand why he should be out in the cold when he wasn't the one who had tried to escape. When head counts on each wing started, Francis's heart started to race. The officers were angry, and Francis knew how dangerous a force man could be when upset because he was once one. A couple of them had their rifles drawn but pointing to the ground, and Francis knew that they wouldn't hesitate to fire if the need arose.

Silently, Francis prayed that things would not go that far. He had no idea how the UK force system worked and he didn't want to find out. As far as we was concerned, he'd witnessed far too many cases of accidental shootings that led to the deaths of random victims. As the headcount continued, Francis grew restless. He wasn't sure he was standing straight enough and tried to align his posture to that of his cellmates, but as he adjusted himself, an officer slammed a hand on his shoulder.

"You! What do you think you're doing? Step out! What are you hiding?" the officer growled.

Francis wasn't allowed to utter a word as the officer continued to rant angrily, dragging him out of the line and ordering another officer to search him thoroughly. Francis threw his hands up. He had nothing to hide and didn't want to upset the officer further. After several minutes of searching and almost stripping him completely naked, he was pushed back to his line.

"Now the rest of you! You don't move or blink except I tell you to," the same officer barked.

Grumbles and murmurs floated into the air.

"Silence!"

The rest of the guards proceeded to search everyone else and when they were satisfied, they dragged out the would-be escapees from a corner and paraded them in front of everyone. Some of them had cuts on their faces probably from trying to fight off the officers when they were caught. Francis shook his head at their stupidity as it was clear to any fool that there was no point in trying to escape such a heavily guarded prison.

As if reading Francis's mind, James turned slightly to him and said, "They're all in for murder."

Francis's eyes widened as realisation dawned on him. The escapees probably couldn't deal with the idea of being locked up for life.

"Not a sound from anyone!" another officer bellowed, his face hard and cold. "This should serve as a stern warning to the rest of you. There's no escaping this noble prison. You'll only walk through that front gate on bail! Is that clear?"

* * *

The following day, Francis finally received a letter from Agnes asking about his well-being and the situation at his prison. Apparently, the news of the prison escapees had spread far and wide; she was understandably worried and wanted to make sure that he wasn't involved. Francis read through the letter like it was a lifeline, his focus on Agnes confirming her good health and the birth, which was by then two weeks away. Tears blurred Francis's vision as he realised that his long-time desire to be a father was finally about to become a reality. From the 'infertility' in Ghana, through to the miscarriages in the UK, it felt great to have overcome all of that. He no longer focused on the fact that he would not be present at the birth; his sole interest was now in becoming a father.

Francis couldn't contain his joy. He shared the good news with James who had unknowingly become his therapist and confidant. James knew more about him than any other person in the entire country. The man was such a good listener and often encouraged Francis by quoting Bible verses. James was an ardent Christian and had even tried to convert his cellmate, even giving him a bible that he never opened.

Sadly, James was soon to leave. He had been granted bail. Being without James made prison life even more dreary. It then dawned on Francis that despite all the conversations he'd had with James, he never asked James what he was in for. He'd spent the entire time unburdening his soul to a complete stranger and selfishly blinded to the fact that James had his own problems too. Francis was happy that James was finally free, but he couldn't help feeling terrible for not being a better friend, especially as he would never see him again.

17

Agnes had never felt so alone in her life. From the time she was a child to becoming a young woman, she had always been surrounded by family and friends. After her marriage to Francis, he became her family, and in fact, her everything. She had been able to handle the loneliness when Francis was locked up in Ghana because she had Asantewaa and her mom. However, it was different in the UK. For a while she'd thought that she had family in the form of her sisters, but after reading Francis's letters and learning of Adwoa's true nature, she realised that she had no one. She didn't even have Francis anymore because he was locked up.

At night, she craved Francis's back rubs and massages, but in every corner, she turned to, was the hardened faces of women whom she knew nothing about. The majority of them were white, and despite the fact that she shared the same stinky cell with them, Agnes still felt inferior. She couldn't bring herself to interact with them because of the way the thorns of life had entangled her. In all her time in the UK, she'd been disrespected and looked down on by supposed true citizens of the country. And besides, she didn't believe she could trust them at any level, anyway.

Then there was Adwoa. Adwoa, who had betrayed Agnes for reasons unbeknownst to her. So, what couldn't a mere stranger do to her? Agnes was indescribably angry and bitter towards her sister. She was grateful to be locked up because she wasn't sure what she'd get up to when she found herself face-to-face with Adwoa. So, while she was tempted to call Afriyie and tell her that she was soon to give birth, she resisted the urge. What if Afriyie had been in on the betrayal too? After all, Afriyie had never visited her once in prison, nor had she contacted her. Agnes understood that Afriyie was busy at the maternity ward, but so busy that she could not even see her young sister in jail? What was more important than family? Agnes suddenly wished there was a way she could just disown her sisters and never see them again.

The weekly check-up at Willington's was the only highlight of Agnes's new life as a pregnant prisoner. As she sat rooted in one of the chairs in the hospital lobby, she wondered how she'd raise a child alone. Agnes didn't like Adwoa's situation and how Asantewaa had never met her father. She wanted something different for her child and that was a home where both parents were present. A long time ago, she'd promised herself that her husband would be a father to his children in the real sense of the word. Francis had promised to be a present dad too, but circumstances had inconveniently robbed them of making good on their words, and in fact, taken the option right out of their hands.

Agnes was conflicted and it made her weary. Under normal circumstances, she would have first been over the moon to just carry the baby to full term. Instead she was right at the doorstep of giving birth, yet she could not celebrate that either. Instead, she was filled with sadness and a deep hollowness in her heart. She knew that she'd never be happy again until the court case was behind them and they had regained their freedom. All she wanted was to go back home with Francis, so that they'd dance around the living room. As she daydreamed, it dawned on her that all that seemed like a lifetime ago.

The doctor, a white man with thinning grey hair approached her with a soft smile. Agnes couldn't return the smile though.

"Let's go in," the doctor said and offered his arm to help her up.

Agnes graciously took it and muttered her thanks. In the past few weeks, her stomach had grown considerably bigger and heavier. The simple act of walking had become a chore and her breathing was more laboured.

"Everything looks fine. The baby is due next week. I'll write the expected date for you to keep in mind. That's when you should come to hospital or before that if you feel that baby is on the way."

Agnes thanked the doctor flatly, with not an ounce of excitement in her. She'd lost herself when chaos knocked on their front door that fateful evening. The police had almost broken her husband's arm, but he'd survived only to be locked up in prison. Agnes wasn't sure anymore what difference anything made.

"I'll also suggest maximum rest from now on. No heavy food," the doctor's voice rang in her ears.

Agnes nodded, snatched up the white paper he had written on and wobbled out through the open door.

* * *

Back at Holloway, Agnes read Francis's new letter with mixed feelings. He'd suggested some lovely baby names, and one in particular he'd circled, if the baby was a girl. Agnes tried to smile as she read through, but couldn't. It had already been confirmed that he couldn't be with her for the birth. The thought of having to go through the entire birth process all alone made her sad. Consequently, the last thing on her mind were baby names. However, because she knew that Francis was excited and trying to make the most of the situation, she couldn't find it in her heart to deny him that. So, it was with much reluctance that Agnes penned her response.

As she wrote down her true feelings, her eyes welled up, the feeling of being loved regardless of the distance and circumstances momentarily overwhelming her. Francis was like a strong shield to her. He was everything she wanted in a man, as he consistently went above and beyond for her. In that brief moment of deep reflection, Agnes was reminded of how lucky she was to have him as her husband and father to her unborn children. She knew that whatever chaos came their way, she could count on Francis to always love and cherish her. It was just sad that life wasn't fair.

While she thought that she was holding the tears back, one of her cellmates stepped closer and demanded to know why she was crying. Agnes eyed the pale-skinned lady and wondered how she spoke without really moving her lips. Pretending not to have heard her, Agnes dropped her gaze to the letter in her hand.

"Are you alright? Do you need a doctor?" the lady pestered.

Agnes hated how the lady's skin glistened even in the dull light. Nor did she like the way her pale blue eyes made her look like a cat. In that moment, Agnes felt fat and ugly. She sighed heavily and waved the letter. The woman's eyes widened as she blushed.

"Oh, is that from a loved one? I'm sure you miss them," she said.

Agnes knew that Africans loved to gossip, but the whites rarely did. So it took her by surprise that this woman was trying to get into her business. Agnes however had no intention whatsoever of engaging in sorrowful tattletales with a stranger. As far as Agnes was concerned, she wanted nothing to do with anyone who was a part of this system.

The lady shuffled her feet for a few more seconds and then realising that Agnes had no intention of engaging, stalked back to her own corner of the cell. Every one of them had claimed a spot on arrival, and though the two other women had arrived before Agnes and picked the best corners, she didn't mind that hers was closer to the cell entrance. In fact, she welcomed the little sense of privacy, something that was highly fickle in prison.

Agnes shared a large bathroom with over 50 other women. She'd seen more naked bodies in the past few weeks than she had in her entire life. In the first few days, she'd felt incredibly ashamed to uncover her dark, big pregnant body. Her eyes had curiously searched out the women, eager to find someone pregnant like her but she'd come up empty. She didn't only have the darkest skin but was also the only woman carrying a bundle of joy. She had fled and avoided the bathroom for a while, but pregnancy made her skin hot, and she needed all the water she could get to cool her body. Eventually, she got accustomed to baring her body to the multitude of women. The other women seemed fascinated by her big stomach and more often than not begged to feel it. Agnes however, denied every one of them the opportunity to feel her baby kick. She knew her mother wouldn't have approved. Londoners may not practice witchcraft, but as an African, Agnes knew to be extra careful about these things.

When they went to the canteen to eat, some of the ladies offered her extra meat, extra cheese, and extra everything. Agnes turned them all down. She didn't like the attention, and she didn't want to risk being poisoned. Considering the situation, the only person Agnes could trust besides Francis was herself. She'd had her fair share of betrayals, and she wasn't looking to take any more chances.

*   *   *

Francis's anticipation of the birth had reached fever-pitch, so he told everyone who cared to listen that he was soon to be a father. His fellow prisoners shared in his happiness. For the first time since being locked up, Francis was simply happy. He knew that his mother Afia would be ecstatic too. The aged woman had been waiting for a child from him for a long time, and he was glad that he would at least finally grant her that wish.

Over the previous weeks, he'd consistently sent letters to Afia, urging her to lift Agnes up in her prayers. Francis wished he was back in Ghana, back to when he could concoct herbal medicines for pregnant women. He knew that the white men were good at their jobs and that his wife was in safe hands, but he just didn't feel relaxed, especially because he couldn't be at the hospital with her.

However, as Agnes's due date drew closer, Francis became increasingly paranoid. Negativity started to dig a deep well inside him, especially when it dawned on him how lonely Agnes must have been feeling, going through the process all by herself. He wondered whether Adwoa would visit Agnes at the hospital, and that singular thought made him uneasy. Francis didn't want her anywhere near his wife and child. Since he'd told Agnes about Adwoa's betrayal, she hadn't spoken a word about it. He understood that she may be trying to come to terms with the truth, but in the meantime, he couldn't tell what was on her mind. If only he could fly Eno Mmeraa to the UK on such short notice, but he didn't have the capacity. Adwoa or Afriyie would've been in a better position to do that. The harsh reality was that since his arrest, he had no rights to anything, whether it was working, walking freely, or flying people over. He was an illegal immigrant who had been stripped of the little dignity he had left in him.

* * *

Before the arrest, Francis had planned to take care of Agnes for at least three months during her pregnancy. He was willing to take time off work to do just that because as a first-time mother, he understood that she needed some attention. But life in its own weird way had decided to deal them a heavy blow at the worst time. The case was draining in every way — mentally, physically, financially and more. He was losing money badly and was at risk of defaulting on the payments. He knew that he would have to start from scratch when he was eventually released, and that alone made him restless.

He was however glad that Agnes was leaving the crappy prison soon to give birth, and he was hopeful that before the baby was big enough, he may also be released. The night before she was due to leave prison, Francis penned her a love letter. He reminded her of the first time they met, how much he loved her and that he couldn't wait to reunite with her and meet the baby. He encouraged her to be strong for the both of them and made promises about the future that he was eager to fulfil.

Over the next few days, Francis paced every corner of his cell and did not sleep a wink. He had no information about Agnes's condition and there was no letter from her. In his own letter to her, he'd specifically instructed that she write to him as soon as she had delivered. It was now three days past the delivery date and surely he should have heard something.

On the fourth day, during lunch where he had failed to force food down his throat, he scrambled up from his chair and marched to a standing guard.

"Please, do you have a letter from Mrs Agnes?" Francis asked.

The guard eyed him. "I know you. You've been going around asking all the guards the same question. Your wife is expecting a baby, right?" he asked.

"Yes. I'm worried," Francis replied.

The man patted his shoulders. "I'm pretty sure she'll be fine. As soon as we hear anything, you'll be the first to know," he assured Francis.

Francis was anything but reassured, and his worries only compounded as he walked back to his table in a trance.

* * *

Holloway had released Agnes before her due date to allow her to settle in the maternity ward at St George's Hospital in Tooting, where she had been registered to give birth.

However, she didn't like the idea of pacing back and forth in the ward, but she had no choice as she had nowhere better to go. So, with the little money she had left, Agnes got on a random bus and rode it to its last stop and then back again. She did this for a couple of hours until her contractions started, which fortunately happened as the bus was on the way back to St George's.

When Agnes arrived at the hospital, she was soon examined by the midwife. Although she wasn't yet fully dilated, her vitals were very high, with her blood pressure shooting through the roof. Gently, the midwife explained to Agnes that she would have to be monitored closely.

After two days, which was also two days past her due date, Agnes showed no signs of going into labour. She was told that the way forward was to have a Caesarean section. At first, Agnes refused and insisted that she wasn't going to let anyone cut her open. The doctor warned her that any delay was a risk to her health and that of the baby because her blood pressure would become difficult to manage. When Agnes refused again, the doctor spoke in no uncertain terms and told her that without a C-section, there was a real chance that either she or the baby would die.

Those words were a slap in the face for Agnes. She could not imagine the trauma that would come with a stillbirth. The miscarriages alone were devastating, and she knew that losing a fully formed baby would be hell. The cries of newborns in the ward next door drifted into her ears, and she decided then and there that she'd do whatever the doctor wanted in order to hear the cry of her own child. It was that decision that led her to the theatre table that fateful morning of 12 November 1991.

* * *

Agnes went through the motions of prepping for the operation with her heart in her hands. In her whole 30 years, she'd never been as scared as she was then. More than ever, she wanted Francis to be with her, holding her hands and soothing her with his words of encouragement.

"It'll be fine, ma'am," one of the midwives said. She had smooth dark skin and a proper Londoner's accent. Nevertheless, Agnes was surprisingly drawn to the plump lady with a motherly aura about her.

Agnes's heart skipped a beat as her eyes drifted to the bassinet in the corner of the room where her baby would be placed after birth. Her vision blurred with tears. When she had thought about having a baby, a C-section was never part of the plan. Back in Ghana, that was considered to be the lazy woman's way out. Women who couldn't birth their kids the natural way for one reason or the other were made to feel weak and unworthy.

"It'll hurt a lot?" she asked and squeezed her eyes tight, wishing she'd wake up to find that it was all a dream.

Instead, when she forced her eyes open, she was still on the theatre table and very much awake. On top of that, she was now aware of a throbbing pain in her lower abdomen.

"You don't have to worry, ma'am. You'll be sedated so you don't feel any pain, at least until the operation is over," the midwife replied.

Agnes wasn't sure what she meant by sedated, but she had decided to trust all of them. She had no option but to, especially as the various people buzzing around her remained chirpy and upbeat in a bid to allay her fears.

The next thing that Agnes remembered was waking up in a room full of lights, the steady beeping of machines and the soft hum of other equipment filling her ears. Her head felt light, almost as if it were floating, and for a few disorienting moments, she couldn't make sense of where she was. Then, the face of a woman appeared in view, and Agnes could see her mouth moving but could not understand what she was saying. Agnes blinked several times, struggling to focus, until one thing came to mind her baby.

"Where's my baby?" she muttered out to no one in particular.

"We're going to take you to see her soon. We just need to make sure you're OK first. Don't worry, Agnes. She's fine, and so are you," the woman said.

Agnes slowly started to recognise her as the plump midwife from the ward and relaxed a little. Even though her heart was racing, a flood of relief and excitement surged through her. Every second felt stretched, every heartbeat a drum of anticipation. After years of waiting, of imagining this moment, the thought of finally holding her child made her chest ache with joy. She closed her eyes for a brief second, willing herself to stay calm, but the tears that threatened to spill betrayed the depth of her emotion. Soon, very soon, she would see her baby.

Several minutes later, she was wheeled out on her trolley into some lifts and she recognised that she was on her way back to the ward. It took a while for the nurses to transfer Agnes to her bed and make her comfortable. Then the big moment arrived.

"Your baby is coming now, Agnes," said the plump midwife.

Another midwife walked in with a bundle in her arms. As she walked towards her, Agnes felt a rush of happiness and sadness at the same time. Tears streamed down her cheeks as her daughter fidgeted gently beneath the wads of muslin wrap and was laid into her arms. She was of course elated to finally hold her baby girl after nine long months but sad that Francis was not there to witness the moment with her.

* * *

Over the next few days, Agnes began to settle into the rhythm of caring for her daughter. Recovering from a C-section left her weak and easily exhausted, so she had to rely on the midwives to support her each time she lifted the baby into her arms. Yet, even in her fragile state, she cherished every moment, the soft coos, the tiny fingers curling around hers, the delicate rise and fall of her daughter's chest as she slept. She spent hours simply gazing at her, memorising every feature, marvelling at the life she had created. The midwives would gently guide her when she grew tired, but Agnes insisted on holding her daughter herself whenever she could. Slowly, she felt the deep bond forming, and a love so great that it made every ache in her body worth it.

Agnes didn't like hospitals, so about five days after her C-section, she asked to be discharged. The doctor, of course, refused.

"Not yet, ma'am. We need to monitor you and the baby closely for at least a week and then you're free to go."

Agnes reluctantly agreed. The midwives had taken it upon themselves to wash and clean her daughter, insisting that she needed all the rest she could get. Agnes allowed them only because she was not strong enough to do it. Besides, since she would have no one to help her when she eventually went home, it was only wise that she enjoyed the few days of rest. She examined the pink floral baby grow her daughter was wearing and then thought of the baby clothes sitting at home; the home that had been locked up by the police the day they were arrested. The only thing they didn't know was that Agnes still had the keys, and that meant she had somewhere to go when she was discharged.

The other option was going to Adwoa's. As she thought of her sister, anger threatened to overwhelm her. She didn't know if she could ever forgive Adwoa for her betrayal. Francis had been rightfully worried sick about how she would have taken the news, but she couldn't bring herself to pour out her true feelings to him. It was that devastating. It was a real effort to divert her thoughts from Adwoa, but she willed herself to otherwise her blood pressure would have shot up again; it was not worth staying in hospital longer because of that woman. She had more important things to attend to now.

Finally, the week came to an end and Agnes was discharged. It was at that point that it hit Agnes that she was going to be truly alone, and in the colder winter, with nowhere to go.

18

Agnes now stood with the baby in her arms in front of their block of flats. She studied the bunch of keys in her right hand as if they were vipers and wondered if the locks had been changed. After several minutes, Agnes finally walked up the path and pushed open the main doors, which were unlocked, just as they always were during the day. Then, she gingerly walked up the stairs to their flat. After pausing outside her front door to take a breath, she pushed the keys through the keyhole of the front door, turned them, and to her surprise, it clicked open. As she took the first step into the hallway, she was knocked back by the arctic cold, which made her wrap her arms even tighter around her daughter. Pushing the door closed with her foot, Agnes then slumped to the cold floor.

"I'm so sorry, Christabel," she said to the sleeping child.

The name sounded strange to her ears because it was the first time she'd said it out loud. It was the name Francis had chosen for a girl, and the fact that she was using it in his absence made it even stranger. She wiped the tears from her cheeks and pushed herself up to her feet. Then she flicked the light switch on - nothing. The electricity must have been disconnected. When she walked into the kitchen, the stench overwhelmed all her senses. The meal she'd been cooking that evening before the police came sat on the cooker, exactly as she'd been forced to abandon it. The pot, however, had turned charcoal black because she had not even had time to turn it off; that meant there was no cooking gas left.

Scared that Christabel might get an infection from the bacteria that was sure to be swarming around the kitchen, she quickly made her way to the bedroom. There she gently laid Christabel on the bed and sang softly, her lullabies tinged with a melancholy that mirrored her own tired heart. Soon the cold seeped through Agnes's thin maternity dress. She knew that she had to figure out a way to survive this situation. The first thing to do was to keep warm, so she walked over to her closet and pulled out jacket after jacket for herself and two thick sweaters for Christabel. The little baby fidgeted as Agnes dressed her but soon fell asleep. Agnes got out of the now stinky old maternity dress and wore two of the jackets and two pairs of thick joggers.

Christabel woke up a few hours later and immediately started crying; it had been at least six hours since she'd had any milk. Agnes was frustrated. She knew that she had to feed her baby, but she had no money. She hadn't eaten so she couldn't even produce breast milk. At a loss as to what to do, Agnes lay helplessly on the bed with Christabel next to her, and drifted in and out of sleep as she listened to Christabel's cries echoing through the night.

* * *

Morning dawned bright, but Agnes was exhausted from the lack of sleep. The temperature had plunged further, making her mood sour. She tended to Christabel, replacing her soiled nappy with one of the few she had been given by the midwives; that didn't stop her from crying though. Between the cries, Agnes had flashbacks to the time in Ghana, when Francis was in prison. She'd been alone for a while then too, taking care of Asantewaa alone and hopelessly waiting for news of Francis's release; but even then, it had been different and better because she had a family she could rely on. In London, she had no one. The only family she knew had turned into strangers right before her eyes, and the one person she could count on was locked up with no sign of being released. Christabel continued to cry as everything Agnes did to pacify her proved useless.

For the next nine days, Agnes survived on her wits. Breastfeeding continued to be difficult, but she persisted. She worried constantly that Christabel was not getting enough, and the guilt weighed heavily on her. By the first day of December in that winter of 1991, she realised that she had to do something drastic or else another disaster would unfold. Agnes bundled Christabel up and then took the short walk to the local Department of Social Security office where she applied for a crisis loan. The application was processed on the spot, and she was given £10. How she would stretch that she had no idea. In any event, she walked into a small supermarket nearby. The first thing she picked up was baby milk. However, it was so expensive, costing even more than baby food; on top of that, she needed to buy a few basic items to keep herself and Christabel living half decently. Exhausted and emotionally drained, she ended up buying a small jar of baby food and some other toiletries. At least she was left with some change.

Back at the flat, Agnes immediately fed Christabel right out of the jar. As she did so, she thought back to how she had sought refuge at Afriyie's house when the tension at Adwoa's became unbearable. It was her safe space, a place where she could unwind and escape the growing hostility. Maybe she could go there again especially as her need was far greater this time. Agnes decided to do just that and after giving Christabel a few more tiny portions of food she settled her before heading out the door again to Streatham. Afriyie was sure to give both of them a warm welcome especially after explaining the circumstances she was faced with. However, Agnes was in for a huge shock.

*   *   *

Crossing her arms across her chest, Afriyie stood in front of the door, making it clear that baby or no baby, Agnes was not coming into her house.

"You have the audacity to show your face here after saying all sorts of nonsense about me?"

Bewildered, Agnes looked at Afriyie. She didn't understand what Afriyie was talking about. She'd been locked up for weeks, had a baby alone, and all Afriyie could do was talk about old gossip that they both knew was not true.

"Afriyie, what's wrong? Why are you doing this?" Agnes asked in a broken voice.

"You!" Afriyie wagged a shaky finger at Agnes. "Yeah! I heard all about you calling me barren and sorts. All the hateful things you've said about me. Yeah. I heard them alright!"

Agnes blinked back tears, dazed and confused. "How can you believe all this? We were here together when you got that call, remember? They're all lies. Someone is trying to get between us."

But Afriyie wasn't listening and shut the door in Agnes's face. Agnes was left with no choice but to go back to her freezing flat. By the time she walked through her front door, her entire body was numb with cold, and she was certain she'd develop a fever. That night, at least Christabel slept; the food must have filled her, but for Agnes, the hours crawled by as slow as a snail.

After two weeks, Agnes decided that she couldn't take it anymore. She was now in the depths of despair. Her own sister, the one she had looked up to all her life had abandoned her when she was at her lowest. Even as a midwife, that sister had not seen it fit to help her younger sister, her baby sister, care for a newborn. Agnes could feel herself slowly going crazy, and although she kept telling herself to be strong for Christabel, she knew that she was only lying to herself.

Strapping the cranky baby in front of her, Agnes stumbled out of the flat. She got on any bus and just as she had done before, rode it to nowhere. On the bus ride, her thoughts turned dark, and she questioned whether it was really worth living. In her mind, she was simply enduring trial after tribulation; she couldn't even look after the baby she had longed for.

In a trance-like state, Agnes got off the bus at the next stop. It was time to put an end to her misery, so she walked towards the busy road teeming with fast-moving traffic. Just as she was about to step into the road, a solid hand rested on her shoulder and deftly pulled her back. Agnes turned around to see a well-dressed young lady who looked the same age as her. The difference between them was pretty clear, however. While Agnes was shabby, the lady was neatly dressed and stood in complete contrast to her.

"What's wrong, ma'am? Do you know you nearly walked straight into that car?

Agnes did not respond.

"My name is Asher. Do you need help?" the woman continued.

With that, Agnes immediately broke down in tears and right there on the sidewalk, poured her heart out to this stranger. She was tired of bottling everything up, of not releasing the anguish of the last few months. Between the sobbing and stuttering, Agnes bared her soul to Asher, who in turn listened intently. When Agnes was finally finished, Asher directed her to a nearby café and offered Agnes a lifeline.

"You can get help you know, Agnes. There is no need to suffer like this, and on top of that, with a baby in tow. I will call social services right now."

Asher made a call, and with that, gave Agnes a lifeline. She then escorted Agnes and Christabel to an office where Agnes was asked to fill in some forms. More calls were made, and within a few hours, help was on the way. As a new mother with an infant, Agnes was a priority. Just before midnight, exactly nine hours since Agnes had tried to kill herself, she and Christabel were given access to emergency accommodation.

* * *

Asher accompanied Agnes to the flat in Croydon, not far from the Mitcham home she had owned with Francis. It was small with a shared living room, bathroom and kitchen space, but at least she had her own bedroom. Agnes didn't care if it was a hole. The flat was very warm, which was the only thing that was important to her at the moment.

"I'm going to get you some food," Asher said to Agnes. "You sort yourself out while I'm gone."

Before Agnes could object, Asher disappeared.

Agnes looked around the flat. It was functional with plain beige walls and minimal furniture, but the warmth was heavenly — a relief after a month of living in a cold, dark place. Christabel even appeared to sense the change as her whimpering had stopped. Agnes unwrapped her slowly in case she heated up too much and too quickly.

Asher returned about an hour later, arms laden with bags overflowing with groceries and other provisions.

"I can't take them," Agnes said. She was sitting in the living room as Asher placed the bags on the coffee table.

"I insist. You need to eat properly so you can feed your baby. Besides, it's all social services. Why didn't you call for help sooner?" Asher replied.

Agnes was dumbstruck both by Asher's kindness and by the fact that such a service existed. The realisation that without both, she and her precious Christabel would have died that day shook her to the core.

19

Francis heard about Agnes's suicide attempt whilst eavesdropping on two of the guards. One of them he knew had a friend who worked in Holloway. Francis was, as usual, forcing lunch down his throat when the two men started whispering and throwing pitiful glances his way. They had no idea that he was listening even though they had tried to be discreet by using pseudonyms. However, Francis had picked up that Agnes had delivered the baby at St George's as she had wanted to, was discharged and released from prison, then something must have gone terribly wrong for her to want to take her own life. Later on, Francis wondered if they had wanted him to catch on but didn't want to be blunt about it. Whatever it was, the devastating news made Francis lose every atom of hope he had left as he despaired over how disastrous life had been for him and Agnes. He'd always considered his wife to be a strong woman, but he also knew that sometimes being strong was not enough. For her to get to the point of wanting to take her own life meant that she must have hit a dead end. The thought of blaming her for such a decision was tempting but he knew that he couldn't.

Over the next few days, Francis had to put up with whispers in the corridors, fleeting looks from guards who seemed uneasy around him, and the subtle hints in casual conversations reminding him of how desperate his situation was. He wasn't sure why they didn't sit him down and just tell him the full story, straight, man-to-man. He was, after all, her husband and next of kin. What made it even more frustrating was that he had no one to talk to about what he had pieced together.

Whatever the situation, knowing what he knew devastated Francis. How had things come to this point? Francis had fielded every obstacle thrown his way because he knew he had Agnes. What would he have done if he'd lost her? He couldn't even imagine such a thing. Soon, he was consumed with finding out what was happening with Agnes and the baby. During the long days, he sat woodenly on the stone floor of his cell. He couldn't eat. At night, he lay awake and counted the iron bars till the break of dawn. Nothing made sense to him anymore. He didn't know whether to reach out to Agnes because he didn't know what to say. A part of him started to think that Agnes's decision to end her life was simply because she didn't want him anymore. He couldn't blame her, and that sentiment broke him.

To think that he had once been excited about having a family, yet now he wasn't even curious to know whether it was a boy or girl or what Agnes had named the child. To him, all hope was gone; as the weeks passed, he gradually became a shell of himself — withdrawn and thin. His cellmate tried to console him, but Francis was just inconsolable. He truly believed that he deserved everything that had come his way. The one person that Francis did wish was there with him was James. He knew that he might have been able to unburden his heavy heart to him and in return, James would have helped him find a way out. If only they had kept in contact.

It was no surprise that eventually Francis became sick. He was admitted to hospital and underwent extensive examination and testing. All the results were normal, but the consultant in charge of his care was not surprised. He had already recognised that Francis had clinical depression, but it had been important to exclude other physical causes. In the end, Francis remained in hospital for a total of two weeks during which time he received intensive medical treatment and counselling. On discharge, he was given a prescription for mild sedatives to help with sleep and strict instructions to rest his mind. To Francis, that was a tall order, because when confined behind bars, the only thing that one could do was get lost in one's thoughts.

In the days after his discharge, Francis's days had become even more dreary. He was anxious about Agnes and whether she would attempt suicide again, and shuddered at the thought of what would become of him if she did and succeeded. In addition, he fretted over the baby he did not know. He'd made so many plans in his head to give his child the best, but the current situation only told him and the rest of the world that he was nothing but a failure and a barefaced liar. Consequently, the fear of the unknown became his constant companion.

Christmas came and went like any other day. The festivities were lost on Francis. There was nothing to be thankful for and nothing to celebrate in a year that had given him nothing but heartache after heartache and disaster after disaster. Most of the other prisoners had family and friends filling up the visitors' room, but Francis knew that no one would come for him, so he wasn't disappointed. He watched their happy faces with a tinge of envy, the realisation that he had no one hitting him hard.

* * *

The cold that rang in the New Year was horrendous. He felt bare even in his prison outfit, which made him miss the warmth of his home and cuddles with his wife. The hostile environment took him back to his army training days in Ghana, and he found himself revisiting the basic skills of survival. It also reminded him that since his arrival in the UK, he had lost the hardiness and discipline he'd acquired and that had become his trademark.

About two weeks into January 1992, Francis eventually received a letter from Agnes. It was like manna from heaven, and holding the letter in his hands made him feel her presence. At the very least, it meant that she still wanted to speak to him. As he read through the letter, his heart skipped a beat when he discovered he had a daughter and that Agnes had named her Christabel, the very name he'd chosen. For a brief moment, his spirits lifted, filled with pride and joy at the thought of his little one. However, he couldn't help but think about what Agnes had nearly done and realised that he had lost all trust in her. Though she'd written that she would wait for his release, he somehow thought that even if she did, she would leave him soon after. It made sense that she would, as they had nothing to their name and so no reason for her to stay with him. They had gone backwards, right to where they had been five years before. The only difference was that they had another human to care for which only meant additional responsibilities.

In just a matter of hours after reading the first letter from his wife in weeks, and for the first time since his incarceration, Francis dreaded being released. He'd thought that not having a home to return to wouldn't be so bad because he had Agnes; after Agnes's stunt, it was a different matter. He had come close to losing the only thing that truly mattered to him. At least with Agnes he could start again, but without her there was no home, no family, and that was all that mattered to him. Starting afresh didn't make sense to him if Agnes was no longer in his life. Besides, he had come to the UK to grow his family not lose it. The loneliness he felt now was unbearable, but at least he knew she was out there; if she wasn't, how could he even … there were no words to describe the unimaginable.

* * *

Since Mr Ben had been dismissed, Francis had gone through two more lawyers. The big and burly Mr Nicolson had withdrawn his services after realising Francis had no funds to pay the fees. After that, Francis relied on legal aid, which was available even to prisoners without a legal status. By this point, nearly two months had passed since Christabel's birth, and Francis had become increasingly frustrated at the slow progress of his case. He was eventually assigned a state-appointed lawyer to handle his case. In the meantime, Francis only had Agnes's letters to look forward to though they were not as frequent as before. She had decided not to visit because of her precarious legal and housing situation and the fear of drawing attention to her and Christabel. So Francis had to endure long periods of uncertainty about his family.

* * *

Francis did not meet his new lawyer until February 1991, two weeks after he was appointed. He was an Englishman called Mr Riddleston, a sharp, no-nonsense solicitor in his early 40s, who Francis overheard the guards say was known for his meticulous preparation and unshakable confidence in court. He had a reputation for cutting through legal red tape and getting results, which gave Francis a glimmer of hope that this time, the outcome might finally be in his favour.

"I want you to give me every detail about what happened when you were arrested and taken to Kensington Station. We can see if there is anything there that we can use in our favour," he said in their first meeting.

"Well, for one, they nearly broke my arm, and it's a miracle it didn't break," Francis said.

Mr Riddleston briskly jotted things down in a book and urged him to continue.

Francis briefly thought back to how over the last few weeks, he'd almost given up, but Agnes's face in his restless dreams had given him a reason to fight for his life. With renewed energy, Francis gave the lawyer the full story, leaving nothing out. The desperation to leave prison returned with a vengeance, especially as there was no assurance that Agnes would not attempt suicide again. He couldn't imagine his baby girl, whom he'd not even met being taken away by social workers only to be dumped in a strange home. She belonged with them, parents who had prayed and yearned for her for so long. He wanted to go home to her wherever home was. Finally, Francis finished relaying his account to a very patient Mr Riddleston.

"I'll get the rest of the details from the hospital. This should help grant you bail so that at least you can go home to your family."

"Thank you. And let me add that I still have nightmares and constant headaches. As you can see, my right hand is a little crooked."

Mr. Riddleston looked at Francis with sympathy and promised to do everything within his power to shift the case in their favour. With those words, Francis was reassured that, even though they were starting from scratch, this time things would move forward.

After the meeting, Francis rushed back to his cell and excitedly wrote to Agnes, telling her that they would soon be reunited. He wanted to give her something to hold on to. In a way, he was also indirectly asking that she wait for him. He reminded her of how much he loved her even when he knew that love had not been enough. It was all he could give though, and he was willing to go the extra mile to prove it.

20

Agnes had made an effort to settle into the emergency accommodation and was especially grateful for the warmth. However, she was still devastated by her actions and appalled that her pain and despair had pushed her to consider suicide. Had she really been prepared to leave Francis and Christabel to weather the storms of life alone? Even with the help she had received, the pain still dug deep, and so she was plagued with the fear that she could try to end her life again. All she wanted was a permanent balm to her aching heart, but as that was not coming any time soon.

When she received the letter from Francis about his new lawyer and his possible release on bail, she desperately wanted to be happy, but she just couldn't. She was by then way past looking forward to the dawn of a new day. Hope was long gone. Every day felt like a bitter pill shoved down her throat. Taking care of her child was a chore she desperately wanted to run away from. Every time Christabel cried, Agnes felt like she was being strangled.

The social workers continued to offer help through Asher who popped in occasionally to visit. On one such visit, Asher held Agnes's hand.

"Talk to me, Agnes. What's bothering you?" Asher asked.

Agnes fought the strong urge to burst into tears and averted her eyes. "Francis will be home soon," was all she could blurt out.

Asher's eyes widened. "That's good news, isn't it? But you don't seem happy. Why?"

"I don't think I can face him after what I've done."

Agnes was surprised to hear herself confess such a truth. For so long, she'd hidden behind the excuse that she was simply mad at herself, whereas all the while she'd been scared of Francis's reaction to her actions when they eventually reunited.

"Look, Agnes. Francis is your husband. Surely, he'll understand what you're going through. Stop beating yourself up for something that hasn't even happened," Asher insisted.

Asher's persistence only served to make Agnes feel more ashamed of herself. Trying to kill herself was useless and unfounded, and on top of that, she couldn't even show gratitude for all that the social workers had done to help her and Christabel. The only thing that was clear to her was that she wanted to be dead and gone, because there was no way she would be able to withstand another heavy blow. And what was to say another one wasn't around the corner? She had given her all and was tired of everything. The New Year was supposed to ring in a sense of renewed hope and joy. It was supposed to warm hearts, but hers remained ice cold. She couldn't wrap her head around how everything had been going well one minute only for it to upend the next. All her sweat and hard work had been flushed down the drain, and society expected that she put on a brave face. No. Agnes knew that she couldn't. God knew that she had tried, especially for Christabel, but it had been a fruitless effort.

In her depression, Agnes remained in the house like a prisoner, and on the few occasions she went out, she felt that people were looking at her with scorn. To her, the whole world knew that she wanted to end her life and was judging her harshly for that; to compound all that, she couldn't shake off the feeling that she deserved every scorn thrown her way.

"You know what the worst thing is, Asher? I've failed my child. I put myself before this little helpless thing who depends on me," Agnes continued.

Asher countered. "We all make mistakes, Agnes. You'd be shocked if I told you about all the terrible things I went through before I got to this stage of my life. But one thing I'm sure of is that I'm glad I didn't end my life," Asher replied.

Agnes was surprised to hear Asher's admission. It was hard to imagine her having been anything but orderly. However, she didn't push to find out the full details of Asher's life because she didn't want to believe that there was a life that was tougher than hers. As far as she was concerned, her pain and struggles were the worst that one could get, and her actions in response to them quite justifiable. That mindset was the only way she could live with herself.

*   *   *

Agnes missed Francis every day, and longed for nights alone with him when she could simply bask in the euphoria of his presence. However, the longer she thought about his possible reaction to her rash decision, the more fear gripped her — fear that their marriage would end as soon as he was released. Regardless of how life had turned out, Agnes didn't want to lose him. He was all she had in this land that was still foreign to her. Her sisters didn't care about her even after she had turned up desperate, cold, hungry and with a newborn at Afriyie's. There had been no calls or letters from them. Agnes knew that she didn't want them in her life anymore, but the least they could have done was to reach out to the sister they had brought to England. She wanted to vent her anger and frustration at them one way or the other. Being deprived of that very act made her sick to the stomach, and she vowed never to forgive them.

Agnes considered writing to her mum in Ghana and telling her everything that had transpired, but she realised that a letter wouldn't serve any purpose and would instead make the poor woman worry. At night, when the loneliness hit her hard, she played with Christabel and tried to make her smile. Although caring for her alone was a constant struggle, Agnes was truly grateful for her precious baby. She was a sensitive child who cried for most of her waking hours, and Agnes was always stretched to the bone trying to make her comfortable enough to settle. One good thing about that was that it helped to keep the dark thoughts at bay. However, it was so exhausting for her that as soon as Christabel finally settled, she would fall asleep the second her head hit the pillow. Sleeping was the only time that Agnes had to rejuvenate her soul, and she didn't take it for granted because her days were defined by exhaustion and loneliness.

Some of the neighbours tried to befriend Agnes by visiting and playing with Christabel. Eventually though, Agnes became tired of putting up a brave face for them. They didn't know what she had been through and often asked after Christabel's father, but Agnes wasn't ready to share those details with complete strangers; she knew they wouldn't offer any solution and instead would make her a topic for gossip. In fact, Agnes knew that she'd tell her life story to anyone, for that matter. Eventually, she stopped answering the door when they knocked, and soon enough, they read the subtle signs and stayed away.

21

By the end of February 1992, Mr Riddleston's skills as a lawyer had manifested an outcome for Francis even though Francis himself still had some doubts. A date for the hearing had come out of the blue, much quicker than Francis had expected. After languishing in jail for the best part of four months, he could scarcely adjust to the new pace. He, of all people, knew that life could change in the blink of an eye, though he'd become more accustomed to a change for the worse. It had been a long time since things had taken a turn for the better. Before he knew it, he was standing in front of a judge with Mr Riddleston on his left and two of the prison guards behind him. The hearing was swift and sharp, and Francis could not believe his ears when the judge slammed his gavel, signalling that proceedings had ended and he was freed on bail. Francis stood rooted in his chair, gawking at the judge, and it took a firm but gentle nudge from Mr Riddleston to rouse him from his state of shock.

"Does this mean I'm free?" Francis asked the lawyer quietly.

"Yes, Francis. You've finally got your freedom back," the lawyer replied.

Mr Riddleston further explained that although he was free to walk out of prison, his house and passports were to remain in the hands of the authorities pending further investigations regarding his state as an illegal immigrant.

* * *

As Francis returned to his prison cell to get his few possessions, he realised that the house was the very least of his concerns. He shoved his things which included the Bible that James had left him into his small bag, said goodbye to his cellmates and left. The only thought he had as he was led out through the prison gates to the outside world as a free man was his daughter, Christabel. He wondered if she'd taken after him or Agnes, and secretly hoped she'd inherited Agnes's beauty; the anxiety to finally meet her was close to overwhelming.

The buzz of traffic filtered into his ears as he stepped onto the sidewalk. Armed with the address in Croydon where Agnes was living, Francis strode blindly into the road and was almost knocked down by a car. It was because of his quick reflexes that he narrowly missed being knocked over. A slew of curses erupted from inside the taxi, as a black man stuck his head out through the driver's window and spat at Francis.

"Yuh tryin' to die, man!?" the driver shouted.

Francis, still bewildered by the close call, stared at the man blankly. The driver, who looked and sounded

Congolese, carried on shouting and though Francis couldn't understand him, the man's gestures made it clear that he was still cursing. Francis started to apologise but before he could get a word out, the man drove off.

Francis then dusted his clothes off, hailed another taxi and instructed the driver to take him to the address in Croydon. The ride was therapeutic. He'd been shut off from the outside world for so long he had almost forgotten how things worked. He was seeing the streets of London through a new set of eyes. Excitement bubbled inside him as he slipped a hand out of the window to let the chilled air zip through his fingers. Anyone watching him would have thought that he'd been dropped down to earth after years on another planet. He watched a school bus race past, and he imagined his daughter tucked inside the bus and on her way back from school. It seemed all too real now that he knew he actually had a child. It had been nothing but a wish and a dream for so many years, and now she was a reality. Christabel was the fruit of his loins, and he knew that he was going to love her.

He wondered how Agnes would take his surprise arrival. He'd held back from writing a letter to tell her of his release because he wanted to see the surprise on her face when she saw him. Would she be happy? However, he wasn't exactly bothered about that because he knew he wanted to see her, regardless. His feelings toward her hadn't changed, and he still loved her. The news of her attempt to end her life still hit him hard whenever he thought about it, but he wasn't mad at her. He had no right to be angry anyway, considering that he'd left her suddenly, all alone and in her time of need. All he needed was to be with his wife and child because with them by his side, he could conquer the world.

Francis may have lost everything he had ever worked for as a result of his arrest, but this third chance at life meant his zeal to live had come back stronger than ever. He knew that he could only get back on his feet with a positive mindset. Dwelling on the past and what could've been wouldn't put food on the table for his family. He had to get his mind right if he was to rebuild.

As the taxi sped through the quiet roads, Francis thought about a thousand and one places he could apply for a job. When he was in prison, he'd heard that being a waiter paid well, and that one could work multiple shifts; so he settled on becoming a waiter. He'd also thought about going back to the train station to seek out Mr George, the man who'd encouraged him to become a train driver, and beg to be taken back. The only thing was that he was not sure how his old boss would feel about him bringing all his legal problems; one thing about Londoners was that they didn't want anything to do with other people's problems. Being an ex-convict and illegal immigrant, Francis knew that people would give him a wide berth. As he thought through all this, it dawned on Francis that every good connection he'd made since coming to London was as good as gone — he had no one anymore. His in-laws, the people who had brought him to the UK had abandoned him, so how could he expect strangers to do any different.

As the taxi pulled out in front of the address, Francis pulled out the few notes he had in his pocket, paid the driver and eased his way out of the back seat. He stood on the pavement and spent a few minutes staring up at the gigantic apartment complex where Agnes's flat was supposed to be. The knowledge that his child was behind those concrete walls sent an excited ripple through him. He knew that Agnes would be surprised, but the fear of being turned away suddenly reared its ugly head and all the hope he had about them going back to the way things were — when they were madly in love and hopeful for a bright future — rapidly fizzled away. He couldn't go any further, and so he anxiously paced up and down the pavement. Agnes had been driven to such despair that she'd considered ending her own life. He'd failed on every promise he had made to her, and that reality broke him. How could she possibly want to see him? His heart hammered mercilessly against his chest. Then suddenly, his legs refused to budge. He was terrified, but he knew that standing in front of the building was only postponing the inevitable. He sighed heavily, wiped clammy palms down his jeans and cautiously took a step toward the front door of the building.

* * *

Agnes was having a rough day, as usual. Christabel, in her own little world, was fidgety and crying continuously. Agnes murmured tuneless lullabies, but Christabel wasn't having it. When Agnes heard a knock on the door, she assumed it was one of the nosy neighbours and completely ignored it. However, the knock came again, light and firm. Agnes grumbled tiredly and picked Christabel up in her arms. When she pulled the door open, she was so shocked that she almost dropped the baby. Her heart jumped in her chest; her eyes clouded with tears as they roamed up and down Francis's thin frame; her brain froze as she speechlessly gawked at her husband whom she could barely recognise. He looked so different, and not in a good way. Her fingers curled around Christabel's little frame as she unconsciously shielded the child from Francis.

"It's me, Aggie," Francis said, his eyes watching her every move.

Agnes heard the brokenness in his voice, and a fresh bout of pain washed over her. Her husband wasn't the man she remembered from even a few months ago. She knew Francis to be a neat man who took great pride in his appearance. Seeing him with long, unkempt hair and an ugly patchy beard made her feel horrible inside. He'd been locked up for months, and all she had wanted to do was end her own life and take the easy way out. At that very moment, assailed by the visual representation of what Francis had gone through, Agnes hated herself for being ungrateful.

"Kojo," Agnes finally muttered, her lips barely moving.

Francis nodded and smiled, but it was strained. His dark skin looked pale and rough. His clothes were dirty, crumpled and in need of at least two rounds in the washing machine. It took but a few seconds for Agnes to notice everything that was wrong with her husband even as she realised that she was actually glad to finally reunite with him. The worry she had nursed about his reaction to her rash decision was gone. Gently, she pulled him into the apartment and shut the door.

They stared at each other for what seemed like an eternity until Francis stretched his arms out to take Christabel. Agnes hesitated, her fingers tightening on the child. Francis couldn't believe he was finally reunited with his family after so long, and even as he reached out for his daughter, he couldn't take his eyes away from Agnes. To him, she looked even more beautiful than he remembered. He knew that Agnes was wary of him because of his appearance, so he didn't blame her for hesitating to hand the baby over. She did though, and as soon as his fingers wrapped around Christabel, she burst into fresh tears, her small eyes roaming aimlessly over his face.

"I'm your father, Christabel," Francis said as he cradled the baby close to his chest.

"I'm glad that you're finally free," Agnes finally said, through a tear-filled voice.

* * *

Francis wanted to say something but stopped when he realised that Christabel had stopped crying. He didn't want to aggravate her further. Nevertheless, he had so many questions. He wanted to know everything that had happened when they were apart. Had she thought about him when she made the decision to end it all? How could she think about taking such drastic action when he was locked up and looking forward to reuniting with her and their baby? Had she even considered what Christabel would have to go through growing up without a mother? In the end, however, he asked the only question he knew was easy to answer.

"Did your sisters reach out to you?"

He moved to sit on the only sofa in the small room. Quietly, he waited for Agnes's response and played with the sparse curls on Christabel's head. His heart was filled with love for his child, his own flesh and blood. He couldn't believe that there was a time he'd lost hope and thought that he'd never get to be a father.

Back when he was a train driver, a few of his colleagues who knew that he was desperate for a baby had casually suggested that he pick some random lady to have a baby with. However, Francis had laughed the idea off because he knew it was something he'd never consider. His love for Agnes was genuine, and she was the only woman he would ever have wanted as a mother for his children. He had already decided to stick it out with Agnes, children or no children. As he stared into the eyes of his baby, Francis realised that nothing else mattered. He wasn't angry at Agnes. The frustrations of the past few months simply dissolved away, and he was at last refreshed, revived and happy.

"No, they didn't reach out. I don't think I want them to," Agnes replied and sat beside Francis on the sofa. "After what they did, I don't want to ever see them again."

Francis understood exactly how Agnes felt. He'd felt the same way for a while, but at that moment he couldn't care less about them. He'd come to the conclusion that the sisters were just full of hate and would never change. It only mattered that the rest of Agnes's family had consented to his marriage and Charles had stood as the head of the family and given his approval. That was enough. Yes, these sisters hadn't exactly had a say, but did they have to, being so far away in the UK? In the end, they had certainly shown their true colours, and he was certain they would somehow pay for what they had done. Despite their wicked actions, he and Agnes had survived to tell the tale, and now they had the most precious gift of all, and the one thing that mattered more than riches and a house — their first child.

As Francis pulled himself out of his thoughts, he realised that Christabel was in a deep sleep. Her soft breathing soothed him in a way that he could not describe. Agnes was surprised.

"She doesn't just fall asleep that easily, you know," she said. "Let me take her to bed now."

She gently picked Christabel up so as not to disturb her, then took her to the bedroom. Back in the small living room, Agnes returned to sit beside Francis.

"I know you must've heard about what I tried to do. Why haven't you said anything?" Agnes asked.

Francis reached for her hand. "It's all in the past now, and it doesn't matter anymore. You're here. We're finally together, and we have a child, Aggie. That's what we've always wanted. Thank you for bringing her into this world," he replied.

Francis was sure that his emotions were laid fully bare for Agnes to see. He didn't have anything to hide. All he knew was that he loved his wife, and that nothing could quench the fire he carried in his heart for her. He was going nowhere. His home was wherever Agnes was, and he wanted her to know that he was committed enough to keep it that way.

Agnes, however, was taken aback by his response. Francis knew that she was expecting a fight or some sort of contention at the very least, but the minute he had seen her at the door, he knew that he was past all that. The overwhelming feeling he had was one of pure joy.

They sat in silence for a while.

"What about the case?" Agnes asked.

Francis gave Agnes the full details of how his new lawyer had helped him get bail in a short time.

"The case isn't over yet, though. I'll be summoned by the court for a full trial at some point," Francis said.

Agnes's eyes welled up. "I'm so sorry, Kojo. I didn't try to take my life because I stopped loving you. I was so lonely and exhausted and frustrated and scared. I thought they'd never let you out," she cried.

Gently, Francis wiped her tears with the tip of his fingers, his heart breaking to see her so sad. He pulled her closer and gathered her into his arms.

The days that followed the reunion were filled with much soul-searching for Francis. He hated the idea of sitting at home and waiting for the social workers to bring them groceries and supplies. He also knew that getting a job with his current status was going to be a hassle as his months in prison had put a permanent mark on his records; most employers shied away from employing ex-convicts. Besides that, since his arrival in Croydon, news had spread quickly that he and Agnes were illegal immigrants, which meant that they were outcasts and would be treated as such.

Fortunately, Francis wasn't a man to back away from his responsibilities or hide away simply because people didn't like him. As an ex-soldier in the Ghanaian army, this was nothing. He knew that landing a job with the heap of troubles on his head would be tough, but he wasn't daunted. He took the entire situation as a challenge for him to push harder and overcome.

It was with that state of mind that, a week after reuniting with his wife and new baby, Francis hit the streets of London in search of work. He was willing to take on any job as long as it wasn't illegal and could pay his bills. His first stop was at a rundown restaurant. Francis had picked it because he felt that it was local enough for them to overlook his shortcomings, but it didn't turn out as he'd expected. There was nothing for him there, or the place after that, nor the one after that. Everywhere he turned, it was a no. It was as if he had a sign on his forehead in capital letters that read, 'Beware, illegal immigrant and convict here!' Frustrated, Francis summoned courage and asked a potential employer why he wasn't given the job. The mean-looking woman eyed him distastefully.

"Sorry. We don't do blacks," she replied.

So in reality, he was a triple threat — illegal immigrant, convict ... and black. Rejection didn't make Francis lose hope, though. Instead, it fuelled his determination. So he changed his search tactics and knocked on residential homes to ask for cleaning jobs. However, that didn't go well either; some slammed the door in his face and the rest didn't even bothering answering their doors.

Nevertheless, day after day, Francis roamed the streets. One day, he ended up in a really rough corner in a ghetto, where rough-looking men sold hard drugs and wandered aimlessly. There were also a few provocatively dressed women parading around with cigarette butts between their fingers and smoke billowing around their big hairdos. One of the men approached Francis with a promise of relief from his pains and sorrows with just a sniff or a drag. Curious, he asked how much some whitish stuff that promised this bliss would cost, and was shocked at the outrageous amount that he was told. He wondered why anyone would spend that kind of money on fleeting pleasure instead of lasting security. With a shake of his head, Francis cautiously backed away from the unsavoury characters, back to more familiar and safer ground.

* * *

It was now two weeks since Francis and Agnes had reunited, and Francis was certain that they had made considerable progress in overcoming their fears to stick together. They took turns caring for Christabel, and because the social workers were still providing for them, Francis suspended his job search to be present in Christabel's life. He realised that it was an opportunity to make up for all the time that he had been away in prison.

On 3 March 1992, Francis received a letter. Agnes had picked it up from the mailbox and handed it to him. She stood beside him as he tore it open.

"It's from Mr Riddleston," Francis said. "Sit down. Let's read what he has to say."

Agnes sat beside him, and together they read the letter; they were both smiling from ear to ear as they got to the end and looked at each other. The first part of the letter had reaffirmed what Francis already knew — that his bail had been deposited to Horseferry Road Magistrate Court and that he was able to continue staying where he was with his family. The next section read that Agnes and Mr Bakshi had been discharged by the court as the prosecution decided not to proceed with the charges against them. However, Francis was expected to stand trial to close the case.

Relief washed over him, and he was certain that he could handle himself in court as long as he wasn't locked up in a dingy cell.

"Mr Riddleston really is good at his job," Agnes said slowly.

"He has to be," Francis replied.

This was the first time that Francis had genuinely and heartily smiled since his release from prison. He pulled

Agnes up and twirled her around the room just like he used to.

Francis's trial took place within days of the arrival of that letter, and he attended with both Agnes and Christabel in tow. It was a success. In the end, everything had proceeded so quickly, with little fanfare, considering how dramatically it had all started and how much devastation it had caused. The hearing itself had lasted just an hour, and a verdict was delivered the same day: Francis was pardoned based on the fact that in part, he had been misled by Mr Bakshi.

After the trial, Francis offered to take Mr Riddleston out for drinks.

"That's very kind of you, but I'm a busy man, Mr Oppong. However, I hope I don't see you in court again," said the lawyer with a cocky smile.

22

Despite the many months that had passed since his police arrest, Francis was yet to fully recover. He still suffered constant headaches, his shoulders were stiff, and he had limited movement in his right hand. After watching him suffer in silence for weeks, Agnes decided to take the matter into her hands. She pitched a case of police brutality to her local MP Angela Rumbold. For Agnes, the memory of that terrible day remained fresh in her mind, and she wanted to make sure that those involved in harming her husband were brought to justice.

The recommendation from the MP's office was that Agnes was better off taking up the case with the Commissioner of Police. Francis had tried to dissuade her from pushing forward with a complaint, but Agnes refused. One of the things she'd learned from living in London was that if you didn't pay with your money, you'd most definitely pay with your life. For the past few months, she and Francis had paid with both, and almost ignorantly she'd wanted to give her life too. She was extremely bitter about what the police officers had done and desperately wanted them to have a taste of their own medicine. So, Agnes submitted the relevant paperwork, determined that Francis's suffering would be relieved.

In the meantime, Francis resumed his job hunt, and every morning before he left, Agnes helped him massage his shoulders and hands.

"Do you need to go to hospital? Maybe they can give you medication to relieve the stiffness," Agnes suggested.

Each time, Francis insisted that he was fine and left.

* * *

One day, on his way back home after yet another unsuccessful job search, Francis met a young man who was standing by a roadside, handing out flyers. At first, Francis had absentmindedly but politely turned the flyer away, but the man was persistent. Francis then stopped to listen to him, but only out of courtesy. However, the word 'cleaning' grabbed his attention, and after that, Francis started interrogating him further. It transpired that his name was Mr Lawson, and he owned a cleaning company. What took Francis by surprise was that Mr Lawson didn't seem to mind his strong accent, hesitant speech and somewhat limited vocabulary; that alone gave Francis the confidence boost he needed. Mr Lawson then led Francis to a quiet spot where he gave him more information.

Without Mr Lawson asking any questions, Francis opened up to him and told him his whole saga.

"I knew there was something peculiar about you when I saw you. I want you to come and work for me. What do you think?" Mr Lawson said.

* * *

When Francis told Agnes about the job offer, she was over the moon. She even shared her desire to start working too, but the idea didn't sit well with Francis, and he made that clear. As far as he was concerned, Christabel was still too young to be thrown around the streets of London all for the sake of money.

"I'll take care of you and Christabel, I promise. When Christabel starts school, then I'll consider it. I'll work hard for the both of us. With time, all this will be behind us."

Francis started the next day and immediately realised how tough the job was. He was not to be deterred though, because he had finally got a foot back in the door. All he had to do was make it through the first week and apply himself to learning a new way of doing things. Besides, he'd cleaned public toilets, so cleaning homes could not be any worse. By the end of the week, in typical 'Francis style', he decided to take on extra shifts for the following week. As far as he was concerned, he knew exactly what needed to be done and how. Mr Lawson advised him to take it easy to avoid burnout.

"Listen. My friend. You've only been here for a week. Slow down!"

Francis laughed it off. "I've always been a hard worker," he said.

And so for the next few weeks and months, Francis worked himself to the bone. However, his pay did not compare to what he had earned as a train driver, and although he was grateful at first, he soon started to resent his menial job. He'd been in London long enough to know that the money he was getting was nowhere near what he needed to move his family to better accommodation, much less to owning a home. He desperately wanted to move past his poor situation, and when he realised how long it would take for that to happen with the work he was doing, he slowly lost interest and motivation and started slacking off. On one occasion, he forgot to clean an entire room and on another, spent the entire shift doing nothing but staring at the floor. Twice, Mr. Lawson called Francis to his office.

"What's going on, Francis? This is the fifth complaint this week," said Mr Lawson.

Francis heard his boss clearly, but he couldn't find the words to explain himself. Everything was jumbled in his head, and it was on his way home that he realised that he was losing his mind. That realisation shocked him — to know that depression and frustration were eating him up. What made it more frustrating was that he didn't know how to pull himself out of the darkness or step out of the mindless loop. Even being at home brought little relief. He very much enjoyed the evenings at home with Agnes and Christabel; those few hours with his girls before bed were precious. However, with his mind going haywire, he no longer found solace in that. He practically stopped talking with Agnes and completely ignored her when she tried to reach out.

* * *

Agnes, on the other hand, had been full of excitement when Francis first returned to work. For her, it felt like they had finally moved on to a new chapter in their lives, and one that promised stability. Their reunion after all the turbulence, coupled with the steady rhythm of family life, gave her hope. She and Francis had fallen into a routine that made her feel secure. Caring for Christabel together brought her joy, and she often thought back to the first time their daughter had slept peacefully in her father's arms, as if she too had recognised that Daddy was home at last. Daytimes were easier. She'd settled into her role as a mother, finding comfort in small rituals — feeding, bathing, and walking Christabel around the flat. It was the evenings that brought her the most joy, and once again, it became her favourite time of the day. Francis would return from work, Agnes would hand Christabel over, and for a while everything felt right. Slowly, she began to notice the change in him creeping into their lives without warning. Francis grew quieter. He would sit in silence, retreating deeper into himself. At first, Agnes told herself it was fatigue, but soon she realised it was more than that.

"Francis, talk to me," she urged one evening as she laid Christabel in her cot.

"I'm fine. Just leave me alone," he muttered, not even looking up.

His words cut her, not because they were harsh but because they were hollow. She recognised the emptiness in his voice, and it reminded her of her own depression, when she had felt the world caving in. For a fleeting second, she wondered if her husband was slipping into the same pit she had once known.

At her best, Agnes was not one to sit back. She remembered how she had taken matters into her own hands before and got a result. Now it was time to do the same. The complaint that she had made against Kensington Police had been taken seriously. Just as Agnes had noticed Francis' mental deterioration, a letter had arrived informing her that a hearing on the matter had been scheduled for November 1992, just a short three months away. However, with things as they were on the home front, Agnes had not been able to discuss a plan with Francis. All she knew was that in order to win that case, she had to fix Francis. Something had to be done.

23

In the months leading up to the hearing, Agnes focused on getting her husband mentally prepared for the hearing. She cooked his favourite foods and took him out for walks with Christabel. They started to have more deep and meaningful conversations as they reflected on how far they had come. October was coming up, the month marked one year since their imprisonment, a painful reminder of all that had been lost. Yet soon after would be Christabel's first birthday. That is what they chose to focus on, and so decided that a celebration, no matter how small, was necessary.

For the occasion, Agnes baked a simple sponge cake and set a single candle on top. She also made some of their favourite Ghanaian meals. Francis managed a smile as Christabel clapped her hands and giggled at the flickering flame, and for a brief moment Agnes dared to believe that he was coming back to himself. But later that night, when the house was quiet, his silence returned heavier than before.

*　　*　　*

At the end of November 1992, Francis made his first appearance at Southwark Crown Court where his case against Kensington Police was heard. The state-appointed lawyer argued his case eloquently for the duration of the trial. After a few days, the verdict was in, and it took both Francis and Agnes by surprise — perhaps less so for Agnes. The judge ruled in Francis' favour, and Kensington Police were found guilty of using excessive force as well as causing bodily harm. Agnes was ecstatic, and although Francis wanted to be happy, he just couldn't muster the will to show any reaction; his emotions were by then totally blunted by depression. Agnes brushed it off — even though she knew how bad her husband had become. She was hopeful that the good news would change his mood; he just needed time. Maybe their first Christmas as a family of three would do the trick.

*　　*　　*

Agnes tried her best to make the festive period a special one, hanging paper decorations and preparing the fanciest meal she could with what they could afford. As they sat together on Christmas day, Francis focused on Christabel as she tugged at the shiny wrapping paper instead of the toy that came with it. She could see that her husband was willing himself to enjoy the moment, but at the same time, she could see how distant he was and heard how forced his laughter sounded. To her, Christmas symbolised survival and new beginnings. To Francis, it was only another reminder of the heavy burden that he carried. Agnes knew she would have to seek professional help soon, but she wanted to give him more time, wary that Francis might be institutionalised again. She didn't want that for him again.

* * *

Regardless of what Agnes wanted, Francis's depression continued to worsen. Not long after the New Year, he just stopped going to work, without a word to anyone. His days were spent tirelessly pacing up and down the small room. Clueless as to what had happened and scared that he might have lost his job, Agnes made her way to Mr Lawson's office where she discovered something surprising.

"Mr Francis quit. He said he was done with working for peanuts," Mr Lawson hurriedly explained. "It put me in a tight spot to be honest, as he was one of my best. I'd be happy to have him back to be honest with you, but in the meantime, I have to replace him.

Agnes was speechless and could only mutter a soft 'thank you' to Mr Lawson before leaving. As she made her way back home, a strong urge to run away engulfed her. When Francis was in prison, she'd desperately missed his company, and when they had reunited, she thought everything would go back to the way it was. On the contrary, things had worsened, and she finally had to accept that her way of fixing things was not working. One thing that had been a constant with Francis was that he loved to work and provide for his family. For him to quit without good reason, and not even tell her, meant that things were bad. Something was twisting his thinking. She knew the Francis who was a disciplined and ambitious man that had survived the brutality of the Ghanaian army and being dehumanised in a British jail, when all he had wanted was a better life for the both of them. She yearned for the Francis who still held a deep love for her even after she had disappointed him by nearly taking her own life. This Francis, she didn't know, and she felt helpless because she had run out of ideas to make him better.

* * *

After two months with Francis languishing at home, Agnes decided that she'd had enough and decided to speak to Asher. They hadn't spoken for some time as Asher had told Agnes to take her time to bond again with Francis and Christabel.

"If you need me for anything, just say and I'll be right there. You know that," she'd told Agnes.

So it was no surprise when Asher turned up at the Oppong's flat soon after Agnes's call. Asher took one look at Francis and knew that it was a crisis.

"Agnes. Francis needs to go to hospital," she said firmly. "And right now."

She made a phone call, and Agnes could hear her talking hurriedly, saying things like 'clinical depression' and 'major depressive episode' and 'stress'. Within an hour, a doctor and a social worker arrived at the flat. They tried to speak to Francis, but he sat motionless, staring into space. After a brief exchange with Asher and Agnes, the doctor nodded gravely and said that Francis needed immediate hospital care. An ambulance was called.

"My husband is not mad," Agnes insisted even as Asher explained the situation.

"Agnes. That is not what I'm saying. This is a medical emergency. Look. Francis is not even answering my questions. No eye contact. Nothing. This is depression, and it can be treated."

Agnes didn't know what Asher was talking about, but deep down she knew something had to be done.

Within hours, Francis was admitted to Springfield Hospital, a psychiatric unit in Tooting. There he underwent a long examination whilst Agnes waited with Christabel and Asher in a large but warm waiting room. She cradled Christabel who for the first time in a long time was fretty and unsettled. Fortunately, Asher was able to take Christabel periodically to give Agnes, who was also very anxious, a break. Finally, a nurse came out to tell them that Francis had to be sectioned. Agnes was shocked, and so even though the nurse gave her a full explanation of what that meant, she did not take anything in.

"Yes, Agnes. But the hospital will take care of him. Six weeks will be over before you know it," Asher replied.

"Can I see him before we go?" she asked the nurse.

"Yes, but you have to be quick as we need to get his medication started so that at least he can sleep. He's exhausted."

With that, the nurse led Agnes through some double doors, down a long corridor and past several rooms before coming to a stop at the end. Agnes couldn't believe that each and every one of the rooms was occupied. It crossed her mind that they must all have been mad like Francis, and the realisation that so many people suffered like this disturbed her greatly. Francis's room was at the end. As she walked in, she looked at him solemnly as he sat upright on the metal-framed bed, stiff as a rod, eyes staring straight ahead. He didn't even sense her presence as he normally would have done. She watched as another nurse coaxed him to take some tablets, which he just about managed to swallow.

"Go on," the first nurse told her.

Agnes moved to his bedside and stroked her husband's hand.

"Everything will be fine, Francis. You'll be back home soon, and don't worry, I'll be there."

She wasn't just saying that for his sake but also for hers. A whole six weeks without him was unimaginable for her at that point, but she could not have said otherwise.

As she walked out of the hospital with Asher and Christabel, and all the way back home, using all her might, she convinced herself that it wasn't such a long time to wait. She also consoled herself that at the end of it, at the very least, Francis would surely be better than he was then.

* * *

At home, Agnes quickly fell into a new routine. She fed Christabel, cleaned the flat, and managed the meagre funds she had, all while trying to hold herself together. The flat was quiet and sometimes oppressive, yet she felt a growing sense of resilience. With Asher's support — her checking in, offering advice and helping with errands — Agnes discovered that she was stronger than she thought. She could manage the home, care for Christabel and navigate the chaos of her life, even in Francis's absence. Weekly visits to the hospital allowed her to see Francis briefly, though he remained largely unresponsive, sitting in a corner, staring blankly. Each visit was a mixture of hope and heartbreak.

The hospital was a blur of pale walls, murmuring voices and the constant hum of activity. Francis's mind felt trapped in fog. Therapists, doctors and nurses came and went, each trying in their own way to reach him. Some days he barely spoke; other days he wrote short notes to Agnes, assuring her he was still there. Slowly, fragments of the man he was began to piece themselves together spurred on by things as simple Christabel's laughter.

* * *

Finally, one sunny day in May 1993, Agnes received the phone call she'd been waiting for. On the other end of the line was one of Francis's key nurses, telling her that Francis was ready to be discharged and that they could take him home when they were ready. Agnes immediately rang Asher who left work early to pick Agnes and Christabel up for the drive to Springfield.

They made the journey in silence though when they walked onto the ward, both women were as anxious and excited as each other. Heart pounding, Agnes was led into Francis's room with Christabel taking little steps beside her and Asher close behind. As soon as Francis saw Agnes, his eyes softened, and a faint but genuine smile appeared. Christabel, now 18 months old, ran up to her father, climbed into his lap and clung to him as if sensing the significance of the moment. Agnes felt a surge of relief; the Francis she knew was finally back. An hour later, armed with all the medication that he needed, Francis walked out of the hospital with Christabel in his arms, his wife by his side and with Asher as their trusted friend to take them back home.

As soon as they walked into their room back at the flat, Agnes could feel that the mood was already lighter and brighter. Though Francis had not said much, he exchanged giggles with Christabel continuously and even offered to put her to bed. In any event, she would not have let go of her father, the way she was nestled in his arms. After she had fallen asleep, Francis joined Agnes in the living room where they had their first meal together in three months. She could tell that he was not ready to talk about his time in hospital, and she did not push him to. He was more comfortable hearing about Christabel, how much she had grown and what she had learnt to do whilst he was gone. After dinner, Agnes ensured that Francis took his medication as instructed before they retired to bed. Both husband and wife slept soundly for the first time in a long while.

In the first week since his discharge, Francis allowed himself to bask in the simple joy of being home. He enjoyed looking after Christabel, allowing Agnes a much-needed break after months of effectively being a lone parent. Gradually he opened up to Agnes though much of the conversation was centred around him going back to work. She knew that she could not hold him back from work for very long; her husband's identity was tied into him providing for his family and being of use to society — even if it was in a society that did not value him. Asher dropped by frequently in those first few weeks too to make sure that the reunited family remained on track to a full recovery. She was well aware that the risk of relapse of depression was highest in those early days after discharge, and she didn't want that for them. They had been through more than enough.

Agnes could see that it was now time for Francis to get back to work; she could no longer convince him otherwise. In any event, part of his rehabilitation was getting back to the things he enjoyed doing, and when at his best, Francis enjoyed. working. Fortunately, Mr Lawson had stayed true to his word, and on the day that Francis walked into his office, he welcomed him back without a hint of hesitation. The only thing he asked of Francis was to promise to ease himself back in slowly and, in fact, would put a stop to any extra hours if he felt that Francis was not coping. Francis had no objections because he was just happy to be back with the business. He also started to develop an appreciation for balancing work with evenings focused on Agnes and Christabel. Though he was still cautious, he also started reconnecting with the outside world. He still wasn't as jovial as he had been, and for a while, the only friend he had was Agnes.

With the newfound peace in the household, the months flew by. Agnes found a new level of strength and leadership that she didn't know she had. Francis's recovery was nearly complete. His mood had stabilised, and the low moments became less frequent. To ensure that he did not become overwhelmed, Agnes continued taking the lead in many areas for some time. Francis in turn quietly marvelled at how his wife managed Christabel's growing needs and the household with competence and patience. Nights were more peaceful as Christabel slept more peacefully in her father's arms. Agnes took comfort in these small victories, feeling more in control of her life than she had in months.

24

In June 1994, a year after his discharge and full recovery, Francis and Agnes finally got news that they would be rehoused to a bigger flat on Pawson's Road, which was not far from where they had lived. Even though it was going to be temporary, at least there would be more space and an opportunity to start again. As was usually the case with state housing, they had to move almost immediately. Fortunately, as they did not have a full home to pack, the move to the new flat was smooth. Asher was on hand to help them, and in fact, her car was big enough for all that they had.

It was so liberating to have more space and, for the first time in two years, a place they could turn into a home. The new flat had an extra room, and they no longer had to share living and kitchen space with others. As they remained in the same neighbourhood, there was minimal upheaval in their routine. Francis was now on an even keel at work, and the last thing he needed was a longer commute to work. It meant he could continue adding more hours and extra duties without eating into his family time. He was now responsible for training new staff. When he got home, he took over Christabel's evening routine, after which he would make time to sit with Agnes and tell her about his day. Agnes looked forward to his stories as she had little contact with others whilst at home caring for Christabel.

For the first time in a long time, Francis was able to look Agnes squarely in the eyes and open himself to her; they talked about anything and everything, just as they had done back when they were newlyweds. When Agnes was sharing news of her day and Christabel's latest antics, Francis could not help but think about how close he had come to losing everything he loved. Whilst at Springfield, he'd fought hard to find himself — to get his mind right as he called it — because he knew that his family depended on him. Above everything, he wanted to be present in Christabel's life. It had been a driving force for him since her birth, and he was determined to give her his best.

"Christabel's growing so fast, and she's such a beauty," Francis said to Agnes one Sunday evening as he put the little girl to bed. He marvelled at how the small little thing he had met nearly two years before was slowly filling her cot bed.

"She takes after her mother," Agnes replied with puffed-up shoulders.

"Last time you said she takes after me," Francis reminded Agnes as he returned to sit on the couch beside her.

"Your stubbornness, yes. Everything else is from me," she retorted playfully.

They shared a quiet laugh, mindful not to wake Christabel because she was going through a phase of sleeping lightly. As they stared into each other's eyes, memories of their previous life flashed through Francis's mind. There were his childhood days, when he'd run through the entire house just to escape from the whips of his older siblings. His stubbornness had first reared its head when he'd turned his back on becoming a herbalist and instead joined the army that nearly claimed his life. Despite that, he was certain that if given the chance to turn back the hands of time, he'd still become a soldier. It had given him a sense of responsibility and independence from a young age, and that is what had pushed him through all the difficulties he'd faced. Although he had ended up as a wanted criminal in the country he had served faithfully, he was still proud of what he had achieved and the sacrifices he had made.

* * *

In the months that followed the move, Francis and Agnes continued to build on their bond and raise their child. Slowly, the dark cloud that had settled over them start to lift, but they both still could not think of the future; in many ways they were scared to, because one harsh lesson they had learnt was that you never knew what tomorrow would bring at your door. Without realising it, they had settled, albeit tentatively, into where they were and who they had become. Though they often thought back to their days in Ghana, it all seemed a lifetime away, and sometimes it was better not to dwell on those memories because it would not change their current situation.

However, Francis did start thinking about how he could resume supporting his family back home. It was a small, cautious thought, but one that hinted at a tentative return of hope and a sense of responsibility beyond the walls of their flat. The timing was right because towards the end of the year he received a letter from his big brother George that their mother Afia was sick. Although the details were scanty, there was enough there to help him deduce that she had been sick for a while and had recently deteriorated. The gravity of the situation was clear and sat heavily on his heart. He desperately wanted to be in Ghana to treat his mother with the herbal remedies that Yaw had diligently taught him as a boy. That made him think of his father for the first time in a long time, and how he had also missed being able to heal him with the knowledge he'd bestowed upon him. In all that he had gone through, Francis had somehow never given up on the idea of one day sending for Afia. He wanted her to meet her grandchildren and experience a life that was different from Ghana. Now, the hope of that ever happening had started to fade. For the first time in a long time, Francis sent prayers to heaven, pleading that Afia be spared the mark of death. When Yaw died, he'd lost a huge part of himself. Now, if Afia died, he would be an orphan, and that was too big and bitter a pill to swallow. He had never thought of losing her. Of course, he knew that she was getting older, but no one, no matter how old, ever thought of their mother dying. Mothers are always there. Although his siblings were still alive, he knew that there was only so much they could do for him because they had their own families to worry about, just like he had Agnes and Christabel to think of.

"I'm sure she'll be fine," Agnes said after he showed her the letter.

Francis nodded, a heavy lump lodged in his throat. He knew that Agnes was consoling him in the way that any wife would; he was already sure though, in his heart of hearts, that the next letter that came would say otherwise. Nevertheless, he welcomed her soothing words, even in the knowledge that they brought temporary relief.

When the news of Afia's death came a few weeks later, Francis wasn't surprised, but he wasn't any less heartbroken. His siblings promised to handle everything regarding the burial in his absence. Though he was not in a position to have done much, it made Francis feel left out, just as he had when Yaw died. In fact, he'd always felt left out of everything since he was born, and with so much distance between him and his family, the feeling was now worse. He was torn and broken.

Francis followed the Ghanaian tradition of wearing black during the mourning period, which typically lasted **40 days** in Muslim families like his. Although he had been exposed to Christian practices in prison through his cellmate James, he remained connected to his

Muslim heritage. Wearing black allowed him to honour his mother's memory, making him feel connected to her. He asked that Agnes and Christabel do the same because he wanted them all to feel a part of the send-off for Afia, especially as they couldn't be there in person. His mood naturally plummeted, but both he and Agnes recognised and accepted this as a natural reaction and part of the grieving process.

He also continued to work. When Mr Lawson recognised the change in his demeanour, forcing Francis to share the news of his mother's death, he offered his condolences and gave Francis a few days off; Francis, however, refused. He knew that staying home would only give him time to think about his loss, the 'what-ifs' and the 'if-onlys'. The fact of the matter was that nothing could bring his mother back, and so there was no point in 'wallowing in self-pity', as he called it. Working kept his mind occupied and the painful thoughts at bay for most of the day. Deep down though, he knew that he did not want to go back to the depressive state he had sunk into before.

The mourning period came to an end, and gradually, Francis returned to his usual self. Christabel was more of a motivation than ever before especially now that he knew what it felt like not to have the security that came with knowing your parents were still around. As a result, he doubled down at work. Mr Lawson did not fail to notice his renewed vigour and as a result, appointed him to officially oversee a new batch of employees. It wasn't a major promotion, but to Francis, it was a big deal and a boost to his confidence. He didn't take Mr. Lawson's trust in him for granted, so he launched himself into his new role with gusto. The new position massaged his ego somewhat, especially with the pay rise that came with it, but he knew that the responsibilities would increase.

Francis thought back to when he had returned from Springfield with his life seemingly hanging on by a thread. He'd never imagined that things could have turned around as they had done. The thing that was now certain in his mind was that whatever predicament he was to find himself in, getting out of it was down to him and him alone. He was the only one who could determine the course of his life; once he held on to hope and remained resilient, he knew that he could overcome the storms that came with life. Francis reflected on his own personal storms and recognised that those troubles had led him to this realisation, and so he was committed to soldiering on with purpose. He became even more dedicated to Agnes and Christabel, stopped yearning so much for the past and worrying less about the future, so that he could savour the time with them. It was this renewed sense of purpose that carried him through the rest of that year, up to Christabel's third birthday and followed by Christmas. It was to be the first time that Francis was able to really get into the spirit of the season. In fact, he was determined to take it up a notch or two, and he kicked things off by first taking a whole week off to celebrate Christmas and ring in the New Year of 1995.

"I think we should have special outfits for the New Year festivities just like we used to do it back in Ghana," Francis said to Agnes.

"Are you sure? We've never done that since coming to London," Agnes replied. "Where would we even start?"

Francis responded with a smile. He knew how easy it was to ignore the festivities when outside the shores of one's homeland; the usual excuse was saving money, which sadly meant that things that were once routine became luxuries. However, when he was a boy, even with the little they had, there was never an Eid al-Fitr or New Year that went by without traditional celebrations. He never heard his father complain about the family buying new clothes and preparing feasts, and for those reasons and more, he was grateful to Asantewaa for making his childhood so joyous. Now that he was a father, he wanted to do the same, in fact better, for Christabel. Life was just so short — in what felt like no time, he'd lost both parents. And life waited for no one either. One thing that being in Wormwood Scrubs and Springfield Hospital had taught him was that life will always go on without you. It never stopped a measly second for anybody. So, it was either you moved in tune with life or got left behind, and he was tired of getting left behind. It was now time to move with big and bold and forward strides. Plenty had happened in his absence, and he wanted to make up for the times he hadn't been there, in one way or the other, starting with making memories and creating a life with his family.

Francis was also done with limiting himself. All the money he'd saved from his hard work was gone, sucked away by lawyers and the courts. The only evidence of how much he had once made in London was the house he'd bought and which was still in police custody. He didn't know when or if he'd get it back. Regardless, he decided to no longer be held hostage by things that he couldn't change in a bid to keep that promise to himself of moving forward.

With the help of some of the neighbours, Agnes and Francis found a local fashion designer to make *ankara* outfits for the whole family. They were beautifully and perfectly made, and when they tried them on, the couple were transported back to their days in Ghana. When New Year's Day finally came, Francis's heart was full. Agnes took to the kitchen and made several sumptuous Ghanaian delicacies that he hadn't had in a very long time. African food was very expensive and considered a luxury, but Francis didn't care. It was more important that Christabel got a chance to experience what they had as children and that her parents were there to watch her enjoy the experience. Ghana was in their home. To Francis, Agnes had never looked so happy. He felt proud knowing that he'd brought back the sparkle in her eyes. The past few years had been filled with so much pain, and he'd felt like a failure. Now, he was finally back to being the head of the family, and it gave him such satisfaction to know that he could take care of his family.

25

As winter turned into spring, Agnes revisited the subject of going back to work and but the idea, as usual, didn't sit well with Francis.

"It's still too early, Aggie. You've taken care of Christabel by yourself all this time. I'm back to myself now. Let me take care of the both of you for another year at least, and then maybe I can reconsider," Francis said.

Agnes wasn't convinced, but she let the issue rest and in her mind, decided to return to it later.

Francis's desire to take care of his family was indeed earnest, but it wasn't all there was to it. The real reason behind his lack of enthusiasm at Agnes returning to work was his fear for her. Agnes had lost two pregnancies when she was in full-time work. He couldn't imagine the strain that working *and* taking care of Christabel would put on her. Agnes's health was more important than a few extra pounds, and he certainly didn't want the family to experience another miscarriage when he had a job that paid all the bills. For the first time since he'd started working, Francis was content. He realised that he'd started off as a pretty greedy man, working non-stop and trying to do a thousand things at the same time, just to get enough money to buy a house, only to be thrown back into the streets. He'd even wanted to buy a car at one point, but he'd put that to rest. He'd learned his lesson and had chosen to be grateful for the little he had. Francis was truly done with the hustle and bustle of life in London, and he didn't want Agnes to get into it again. He knew she wouldn't understand if he explained it to her, so he kept his mouth shut.

However, a few weeks later Agnes, just as she had planned, raised the subject again, and this time with more pressure.

"I'm tired of staying home, doing nothing. All the wives around here work. Christabel is going to be four this year, and she doesn't need me as much anymore," Agnes said.

Francis sighed heavily as he thought about the best way to approach the situation. He knew that once Agnes made up her mind, it was difficult to get her to do anything else. In fact, she'd picked an opportune time, late at night, waking him up to express her frustration. Francis knew that this was a clear indication that refusing to agree wouldn't work. In fact, she was no longer discussing the matter — she had made the decision and getting his agreement, even if it was by subtle subterfuge, was a mere formality.

"Yes, Christabel will soon be four, but right now, she's just a toddler. Do you plan to take her to work every day? I'm pretty sure no employer will condone that. And I don't want her being left in the care of strangers. I don't trust these people," Francis said.

"Don't worry about that. Christabel will start nursery. All the neighbours' kids go to nursery," Agnes replied.

Francis was surprised to see that Agnes had everything figured out, but he didn't like the fact that Agnes was comparing their life with those of their neighbours. Despite having come to terms with all that had happened, he remained wary of people. However, he had no counter-strategy especially as he had only focused on ignoring the fact that at some point, Christabel would have to leave the safety of home and go to school.

"I don't trust Londoners, Aggie. What if they treat her badly? What if they do something terrible to our child?" Francis countered.

Agnes was not in any way perturbed by his fears and instead reeled off all the benefits of going to school and mingling with other children. After much deliberation, Francis was forced to admit defeat and accept that Agnes was right, so he 'agreed' that she started looking for a job.

Francis' fears for his child weren't that far-fetched. He had firsthand experience of discrimination and racism, and he knew that schools were not exempt from these two societal maladies. He decided not to rely on school recommendations from the neighbours, but instead took the matter to the one man he had come to trust, Mr Lawson. Francis saw Mr Lawson as a mentor and believed in his advice wholeheartedly.

Mr Lawson as usual didn't disappoint as he gave Francis a list of reputable schools that the local black community felt comfortable enrolling their children in. One thing that Francis couldn't get over was that he would not have to pay a penny; in Ghana, growing up, finding school fees had always been a major topic of discussion between his parents and among the adults. It was one thing he was glad he did not have to figure out.

Meanwhile, Agnes threw herself into job hunting. However, much like Francis had when he was doing the same, she became frustrated by constantly coming up empty-handed. Everywhere she turned, she was either told to check back some other time, or that there were no open positions, or that the open position she had seen had just been filled. At one point, she started to think that nobody wanted to employ her, and she was sure that being a black woman was the major reason for that. On top of that, she'd also put on some weight after the birth of Christabel, so maybe some thought that she was not physically capable nor would she be efficient.

One afternoon, she returned home from yet another unfruitful search, and with no Francis to vent to, she ended up pouring her heart out to Ms Maggie, one of the friendly white neighbours, and a divorcee who lived alone with her tiny cat.

"One of my daughters is a manager at that sandwich company. I can talk to her about you in case there's a spot you can fill. What do you think?" Ms Maggie suggested.

When Agnes told Francis about Ms Maggie's suggestion, he was, as expected, less than enthusiastic

"You know how I feel about these people, Aggie. The neighbours know too much about us as it is. If you worked for her daughter, then the whole street will know our business. Besides, I've never even heard of a sandwich company around here. What if Ms Maggie got mixed up? She's quite old, you know," Francis said.

Francis had willed himself to be happy for Agnes if she was to start working again, but he didn't want her to get her hopes high only to be disappointed.

However, Ms Maggie had not been wrong because the following day, she told Agnes that her daughter would be happy to see her. Armed with the address, Agnes took a short bus ride to the supposed sandwich factory. However, when she arrived, she discovered that it was a mere canteen that produced sandwiches for a charity called Age UK. Agnes's hopes of working for a big company with good pay were dashed. Nevertheless, she was greeted warmly by Ms Maggie's daughter, Linda, a cheerful young woman in her mid-twenties.

"You must be Agnes. I'm so glad you could come today," Linda said, giving her a friendly handshake. "We're not exactly a sandwich factory, but we could really use some extra hands. I hope you don't mind rolling up your sleeves."

Agnes smiled despite her disappointment. "Oh, I don't mind at all. I just want to do a good job," she replied. Agnes genuinely wanted to feel useful. She'd stayed home for far too long, and all she really wanted to do was help her husband.

Linda led her through the small canteen, showing her the workstations. "Here's where we assemble the sandwiches, and over there is where we pack them for delivery. Don't worry, I'll show you everything step by step."

Agnes was also able to convince Ms Maggie's daughter to give her a bit of time to finalise the plans for Christabel enrolling in nursery before she started working. Back at home that day, Francis took the news in, feeling a mixture of relief and worry. He helped Agnes talk to Christabel about going to nursery, reading little stories about other children and showing her the routine they would follow. They practiced saying goodbye so Christabel wouldn't be scared, and Agnes made sure she packed her favourite blanket and toy.

In the end, things could not have worked out any better. Agnes took on the morning shifts, allowing her to drop Christabel at nursery and then head over to the sandwich shop. By the time school closed, she was done with her shift and had time to pick her up on the way home. It was the perfect routine that allowed her to make money and at the same time, take care of her daughter.

However, in the first few weeks, Christabel returned from school with complaints about her classmates being mean to her. The situation didn't come as a surprise to Agnes, but she wasn't happy about it. When she had made the decision to send her child out into the world, she knew it was only a matter of time before the bullying started. Even at her adult age, Agnes still suffered unnecessary aggressions because she was black.

Agnes, however, wasn't daunted by the situation and refused to take on a victim mentality. She encouraged Christabel to stand up for herself. As far as Agnes was concerned, this ugly behaviour was something that her daughter was to face for the rest of her life, so it was better she learnt how to control the situation and protect herself from a young age.

Francis, on the other hand, was visibly upset and threatened hail and brimstone. He even wanted to go to the school to tell the kids off himself, but Agnes told him how silly an idea it was to do that.

"It's just words, Kojo. They didn't hurt her. You aren't always going to be there to defend her, and you certainly can't go to her school and confront those kids. You know this isn't Ghana where you can get away with telling off other people's children. You could end up in all sorts of problems. Christabel will eventually grow up, and I strongly believe this is an opportunity for her to learn to stand up for herself, so she won't become a scaredy-cat," Agnes replied.

"Do we have to wait until they actually hurt her? I don't like this, Aggie. This was one of the reasons I didn't want her to start school. She's still too young," Francis argued.

"There's no use running away from the inevitable, Kojo. You and I know that at some point she'll have to face racism. We can't protect her, and in fact the best way to protect her is to teach her how to confront it."

It was a long argument, the longest Francis remembered ever having with his wife in their 13 years of marriage. However, in the end, he realised that Agnes was right. Christabel wasn't going to remain a child forever. Eventually she'd have to come to terms with the bad, the ugly as well as the good of the world, and it was more important that they armed her with the tools to manage all and in her own way. He proceeded to have a lengthy conversation with his little girl where he made it clear to her that anyone who had a problem with black people was themselves the problem.

"Do you know that most people in the whole world have brown or black skin?" he pointed out.

Francis wasn't sure Christabel understood half of what he was saying, but Agnes had convinced him, and his wife was usually right.

Despite Francis' initial misgivings about Agnes returning to work, he was happy when he saw what difference the extra money made. He'd been shouldering the financial responsibility alone for a long time — in fact, so long that he'd almost forgotten how much lighter the load was when they worked together. The extra income helped pay the light and water bills and for a few other things that they had long forgone. It wasn't a lot of money, but Francis was grateful. He even considered the idea of saving again even though it brought back painful memories. When life had been going well for them, he'd been able to put so much aside only for it to be taken by the government just like that. That reminder immediately shut the idea down, and he decided there and then that living each day as it came was the best way ... for the time being at least.

26

In the years since his return from prison, Francis hadn't heard from Adwoa or Afriyie. He'd assumed that they'd reach out when news had got to them that their legal wranglings were over, but he was wrong. It was almost as if the sisters had disappeared off the face of the earth. Agnes never spoke about them, but he knew that she was bottling in the pain they'd inflicted. As much as Francis didn't care about the sisters anymore, he couldn't help but wonder if Adwoa was plotting something else against them. For that reason, he couldn't let his guard down and was extra cautious in his dealings with strangers; for one he avoided arguments and any type of confrontation. Friendships with his colleagues were out of the question, and he kept those relationships pleasant, cordial and professional. Work parties or even drinks were out of the question too.

Francis worked on the assumption that as a black man in London, he was easy prey for the evil machinations of humans. He was also convinced that the government, in their bid to cut down the population of black people coming from the continent, was quick to fault immigrants in order to deport them. Having seen what foreigners did in other people's countries during his army days, he wasn't sure he could entirely blame them, but he didn't like their methods either. To him, it felt sly and underhanded.

It was undoubtedly tough for blacks in London because having to deal with racism and second-hand treatment took its toll. Even in 1995, there were still establishments that operated a colour bar, even though it was no longer as obvious as it had been back in the 1950s and 1960s when there were blatant signs that read, 'No blacks. No Irish. No Dogs.' He'd heard this in the conversations he sometimes had with his train driver colleagues who in turn had been told by their parents.

However, even though Francis faced a lot of restrictions, he refused to be bothered by it. There were more important things that needed his time and energy, and he had no intention of wasting either by fuming over why he was not accepted by all and sundry. Gone were the days when he had just Agnes to think about. Now there was Christabel whose entire life was solely dependent on him, and what he did, and how he did what was needed. He knew that if something terrible was to happen to him, Christabel would bear the brunt of it. Francis realised with clarity that he was no longer living for himself or to acquire wealth, but rather to provide for and protect Christabel and his future kids at all costs. Yes, he had plans for more children, and if left up to him, he would have a whole brood, just like his parents and Agnes's parents had.

"Do you think Christabel is old enough for a sibling yet?" Francis said to Agnes on a cold November evening.

Agnes was taken aback for a moment before she burst into hysterical laughter.

"You want another baby?" Agnes said, tears rolling down her eyes.

Francis felt the heat rising in his face as he nodded. He knew what was at stake, but he only brought up the issue because he wanted to be reassured that Agnes welcomed the idea of having more children. They'd both been eager to have many when they got married, but after the series of miscarriages and the fact that Christabel came by C-section, it was safe to say that having another child had been relegated to a make-believe world and certainly not their real world. Francis didn't need anyone to tell him that the idea of having another child scared Agnes, because it scared him too. He'd heard enough stories of women who went into theatre to have a baby and only one of them came out alive. Francis had no idea what he would do if he lost Agnes, and in reality, if that were to ever happen, it would also signal the end for him.

It was still tough for him to know that Agnes had given birth to her first baby alone. Every time he thought about it, he felt unworthy of his wife and child. However, he had the good sense to relegate that to the past and as an African man, more children was what would make him fulfilled. Although he had no intention of forcing Agnes to have more children, if she didn't want to, he couldn't help but feel entranced by the idea.

"I want another child too, Kojo," Agnes eventually confessed. "And I know the doctor said to take my time, but as soon as I get used to my routine with work and Christabel at nursery, we'll try for another one."

Francis felt a rush of relief wash over him as Agnes's words sank in. They'd never talked about Christabel's birth, but he was glad that she was open to having more children. He pulled her into a tight hug, muttering sweet nothings in her ears. Francis didn't know what he had done to deserve such an extraordinary wife.

"Do you want a boy or a girl this time?" Agnes asked as she pulled out of his arms to look him in the face.

"Aggie, you know by now I don't mind. I just want our kids running around the house and making a hell of a noise, and whichever Allah chooses to bless us with is fine. Christabel would get a playmate too, so she won't always be alone," Francis said.

Although Francis could tell that Agnes, as an African woman who was true to her tradition, was eager to give him a male child, he simply wasn't bothered. He didn't want her to be bothered either. As far as he was concerned, he would cherish all his children equally.

Meanwhile, on the work front, things could not have been any better. After two years back with Mr Lawson, Francis could beat his chest and say that he had made it back. Each time he thought about what could have become of him if he hadn't met Mr Lawson, a chill ran down his spine. He had no doubt that the man was one of his destiny helpers sent by Allah to help pave a way for him. With his many tragedies, they had met a handful of people who had helped him and Agnes, but he was certain Mr Lawson topped the list. The cleaning company was thriving and had grown so much that it was safe to say that they'd taken over half of London as a result of their stellar services. Francis and his team were by then working way beyond Mitcham and were not only handling residential and government buildings but also big hotels. As a result, by the second anniversary of his return Francis' pay had doubled.

"You're my good luck charm," Mr Lawson said to Francis as he returned to the office after signing off another huge contract.

"No, sir. I think you're my good-luck charm. Since I met you, my life has turned right around," Francis replied.

They both laughed.

Even though Francis had changed his perspective, money still gravitated towards him, and so he decided to bury his fears and started saving again. With the help of Mr Lawson, he was able to open a savings account where part of his income was diverted before the rest was sent to him. All Mr Lawson had ever been to him was kind and supportive, in a non-patronising way, and Francis couldn't imagine that there was a time when he had been envious of his achievements. He was ashamed that he could have lost that support to self-pity and jealousy. He also thought back to when his cellmate James had assured him that everything would eventually turn out fine, and he, Francis, had called him a joker. He hadn't believed that an ex-convict would ever get his life back on track and that doom was always going to be his portion. Looking back, all along the way, people and situations had been strategically placed to help restore him to the man he had always been. All in all, Francis was deeply grateful that life had decided to once again smile on him.

* * *

Agnes's work at the canteen was going smoothly. She'd learned how to make sandwiches to perfection and even received a pay rise as a result. Meanwhile, Christabel was growing fast and Agnes looked forward to her chitter chatter as they made their way home on the bus. She was also enjoying nursery more even though the bullying had not completely stopped. The best part of their day was the way she ran to greet her father as soon as she heard the door open when he came home from work. Francis would sweep her into his arms and swing her around the room as her happy giggles filled the house. Agnes saw how much Francis enjoyed their welcome home ritual too. It was good to see the old Francis back, and Christabel had brought out an even more joyful and jovial version of him. Seeing how far they had come as a family filled Agnes's heart with hope that no matter what other troubles life had in store for them, they would most certainly survive.

Francis's self-doubt still reared its head occasionally. One summer's day, Mr Lawson invited the three of them to a small birthday party that he was throwing for his wife. Agnes was surprised but glad he had accepted as it would have taken a lot of resolve for him to break his rule of not fraternising with colleagues. However, on the day of the party, Francis developed cold feet.

"I don't want to go. There'll be all these rich people, and I don't want to have to suffer through their condescending attitudes," Francis said to Agnes.

Agnes had spent the day getting ready. This was the first time she'd had a reason to dress up in several years. In fact, she'd even asked one of their neighbours to do her makeup so that she looked the part.

"What will I do with my makeup, Kojo? Christabel's dress is washed and ironed. Your little girl is excited about all the treats she's going to get. When have we been to a party as a family, Francis?" Agnes argued.

"You can always take off the makeup, Aggie. I don't want anyone looking down on us. We've had enough of that to last for a lifetime," Francis countered as he planted himself firmly on the couch.

Agnes knew she had to be smart about this if she was going to change her husband's mind, so she sat beside him and took his hands in hers.

"You're one of Mr Lawson's best staff. I bet not everyone was invited, but you were, which means that you're special and your presence is important. You keep saying that meeting Mr Lawson is the best thing that happened to you, so why not show him that you appreciate him?

Don't forget that mingling with some of his rich friends may open more doors for us down the line." Agnes spoke firmly and from the heart because she genuinely believed that Francis had been bestowed an honour. Even though he had completely healed mentally, he still didn't fully see his full worth.

Francis shook his head. He understood what Agnes meant, but he couldn't shake the doubt that had crept in.

"I'm just being cautious," Francis muttered after a long moment of silence.

"I understand your fears because they're mine too. But you can't live in the shadows all your life, Kojo," Agnes finished.

With that, she got up as if to say, *we are going* because she knew with her last statement she had got through to him. Minutes later, they were all out the door, with Christabel leading the way.

* * *

The party was not at all as Francis had expected, and for that he was relieved as well as secretly embarrassed for having doubted himself and the type of people the Lawson's were. It was a small and tasteful gathering with a live band playing cool blues music. The spread looked sumptuous too. Mrs Lawson was very welcoming, and the minute they had stepped into the house, she made sure to introduce Francis and his family to the other guests. For the first time in a long time, Francis felt like he belonged, and consequently Agnes also relaxed. When the dance floor opened, every couple trailed on, and Francis took great joy in dancing with Agnes in a space other than their home.

27

As the family's fortunes turned and perhaps because he was now a parent, Francis started to take more interest in the 'system' as he called it. Even though he still maintained distance from anything official and continued to take the view of a spectator on most societal matters, he developed a sort of curiosity in politics especially. In a way, he had no choice because the 1997 general election for the next prime minister of the UK were fast approaching. Every pole on every street in Croydon and the surrounding areas was covered with posters and flyers of the political candidates. Francis had no idea who they were especially since, as an illegal immigrant who wasn't recognised as a citizen, he couldn't vote. Nevertheless, he closely followed the antics and arguments of Londoners as they debated which candidate was best for the country. By the beginning of 1997, the pre-election shenanigans were in full swing. Every channel had some sort of political talk show. Traffic on the roads was heavy as all the candidates took to the campaign trail.

"I'm rooting for Tony Blair," Mr Lawson said to Francis.

Francis could tell from his boss' voice that he was quite excited and wondered why.

"What's special about him?" Francis asked.

"Well, most people are tired of that John Major and the conservatives. He's stayed for too long, and everyone wants a fresh start. Tony Blair will bring all that," Mr Lawson explained.

Regardless, Francis wasn't convinced. He was tempted to tell Mr Lawson that the government and those higher up already knew who the next prime minister was going to be, and that the election was just a front to make people feel that they had a say in the country's affairs. Francis decided against it though, because he could have been wrong. The politics of Ghana had messed with his head so much that he thought corruption was the norm; even though he had experienced the wrath of the system in the UK, things still worked and he had never been forced to flee the land in fear of his life; he could not say that for his home country.

In May 1997, Tony Blair emerged as the new prime minister, winning the election by a landslide. The entire process and the results had captured the imagination of the country. Although the nation had anticipated the birth of a new era, no one had thought it was possible. Mr Lawson was so over the moon and in Francis's mind, anyone would have been excused if they thought that Tony Blair was Mr Lawson's blood brother. Francis had never seen him so excited, and it came as no surprise when Mr Lawson insisted on having drinks to celebrate. The hot weather that day also added to the celebratory mood. There were scenes of jubilation on all the news reports and political talk shows featuring happy people basking in the euphoria of the promise of a new dawn.

"I don't quite understand how all this government stuff works, but I hope Tony Blair lives up to all these expectations," Francis said as he, Mr Lawson and other colleagues sat outside their local pub. He recalled how back in Ghana his people had all but given up on having any expectations of any new leader.

Mr Lawson took a swig of his beer. "Yes, he will," he replied confidently.

28

The halo effect of the election eventually faded, but there remained a renewed sense of hope for quite some time afterwards. Francis continued to work hard, and he and his family grew from strength to strength. It was now 1998, and Christabel had been in primary school for three years. She needed more space, and as Francis and Agnes continued to try for another child, Francis knew that they would soon need a bigger place. Both he and Agnes often watched Christabel with quiet pride. For Francis, seeing her in school uniform, confidently reading her little books and making friends, was almost surreal. He sometimes reflected on how she had once been the baby who would only sleep in his arms, and now here she was, thriving in a world that once felt so closed to him. Agnes, too, marvelled at her daughter's progress; she saw in Christabel's bright eyes the proof that their struggles had not been in vain. To them, every milestone — her first words in English, her first gold star from school, even the way she skipped down the street — was a reminder that despite everything, they were building something solid.

The only thing that stood in the way of getting a new home was Croydon Council housing and its long waiting list. Whenever Francis enquired, the only response he was given was that it wasn't yet their turn to get a house. Agnes, however, wasn't as concerned as Francis was.

"Christabel has finally settled. She has friends, and so have I. Let's wait. I'm sure the council will give us a place soon."

Francis didn't know what to make of Agnes's laid-back attitude on the matter. He had, after all applied for a bigger house because she was the one who had complained that their flat was too small, whilst he was quite content with it.

"Fine," Francis replied as he decided to leave things as they were.

In all his years of marriage, he had learned that a woman was the owner and keeper of the home. As long as Agnes was still comfortable, he too would continue to be comfortable. He therefore set his eyes on another Christmas and New Year celebrating a mix of British and Ghanaian traditions, and he was content in the fact that it was these things, and his family, that made their house a home.

* * *

As the first month of the last year of the 20th century started, the Oppongs yet again entered new territory. Agnes was in the kitchen making dinner when out of the blue, she fainted. Francis was fortunately near enough to hear her faint cry and a soft thud when she fell. He moved swiftly to his wife's side and with his heart pounding away, immediately called a taxi to take Agnes to the hospital.

"What's wrong with Mummy?" Christabel asked Francis as they sat in the waiting room whilst Agnes was with a doctor in one of many cubicles.

"Mummy just needs a check-up to make sure she's OK," Francis said.

In reality, his mind was swirling chaotically, and he had no idea what was going on. All he hoped for was that there was nothing serious going on. Finally, Agnes emerged out of the cubicle and flashed a huge smile as Christabel excitedly ran to her and hugged her legs.

Curiosity was killing Francis, but he knew that the waiting area wasn't the place to interrogate Agnes. Christabel was also too young to hear about whatever was going on. So, he calmly and gently put his arm around Agnes's shoulder and with Christabel, they walked out of the waiting area. When they were out of earshot of all the other waiting patients and their families, Francis asked Agnes how she was feeling.

"A little tired, probably because of the long wait, but I'm OK."

Frances searched her face for any clues as to what 'OK' meant, but he got nothing. In fact, she seemed quite calm, which made him relax a little.

"Let's get you home fast anyway so you can rest. Look, we can get a taxi over there."

Francis directed Agnes and Christabel to a taxi rank where they were immediately beckoned by one of the drivers. Once they were all safely in, Francis held on to Agnes's hand for the 20-minute drive home and said a little prayer for his wife. By the time they arrived home, it was nearly midnight, and Christabel was practically asleep.

"Don't bother getting her undressed, Francis. Just take her shoes off and let her sleep."

Agnes went into their bedroom, and Francis followed Agnes's instructions, especially as he wanted to have time with her to find out what had happened in that cubicle with the doctor. After leaving Christabel sleeping soundly, he followed Agnes and found her sitting on the edge of their bed. She then pulled out a white folded sheet of paper from the bedside drawer and handed it to Francis.

Francis' heart slammed against his chest. He never thought he would feel that level of fear again, but a glimpse of the paper triggered a cascade of emotions that he could not describe. Maybe if he stared at Agnes, her face would give a clue about the contents of the paper because he couldn't open it. However, her demeanour remained calm and gave nothing away.

"Why don't you just tell me what the doctor said, Aggie?" Francis half demanded and half pleaded.

"No, Kojo. I'd rather you find out for yourself. If it makes any difference, it's not bad news. Don't make me ruin the surprise, please," Agnes said.

The fact that it was supposed to be a surprise itself surprised Francis, but it didn't stop his hands from trembling as he unfolded the sheet of paper. His eyes quickly scanned through the words as he searched for one that made sense to him; when he found it, he threw the paper aside and pulled Agnes into his arms.

"Thank you, Aggie," he breathed out as his eyes grew misty.

Agnes dabbed the corners of her eyes with her fingers as she explained that she'd noticed some telltale signs but had kept quiet because she didn't want to get her hopes up until she got proper confirmation.

"Does this mean you'll take a break from work?" Francis asked the one question that was always a bone of contention between them.

He didn't need to spell out how important it was for Agnes to take things easy for the sake of the pregnancy, but he also knew that since his wife had got used to working again, it'd be difficult to get her to stay home.

"The doctor said I can keep working. Besides, all I do at work is make sandwiches, and my schedule is quite flexible," Agnes replied.

"So what did he say happened today? Why did you faint? Is everything really OK?" Francis threw every question at Agnes.

"Yes, really I am. The doctor said it was just a simple faint. All my blood tests, blood pressure and everything was fine."

"That's a relief."

Francis was about to suggest that she took a few days off anyway, but he knew that arguing was pointless.

Besides, from the details on the doctor's notes, Agnes was past the first few fragile months, so he was forced to silently agree. As he and Agnes lay down to sleep, he felt his heart singing. The Oppong Family was growing, and that made him so happy.

Two weeks after the good news, Francis returned home early from work, something he had started doing more of since the news of Agnes's pregnancy. He had long had the room to be flexible since he no longer had to roll his sleeves up and clean every day. So, he figured he might as well use that flexibility to help Agnes more around this house. On this particular afternoon, he received an unexpected call from home. As he paced up and down the flat after the call, he couldn't help but wish that Agnes had been home when the call had come because he had no idea how to break the news to her.

Francis was so saddened by what he'd heard and couldn't understand why it was that every time his family experienced a moment of joy, there was always tragedy around the corner. It had now been four years since he had lost his mother, and although he had recovered, he still remembered the profound sense of loss. Now Agnes had to go through the same thing, and on top of that, in her condition. He couldn't make sense of what life was all about anymore, except that one moment it was all rosy and the next, all thorns.

Francis was so restless that every time a bus drove by, he flipped the curtain aside to see if Agnes and Christabel were coming up the drive. Sadness and worry ate him up inside, and he couldn't wait to unburden his heavy heart to Agnes even though he knew that the news would break her.

The next thing he heard was the door click open, and he knew it was time. Agnes picked up on Francis's dark mood the moment she walked through the front door with Christabel right beside her. As usual, the little girl jumped around, ready to pounce on her father, even with her backpack slung across her back.

"Why are your eyes all red, Daddy?" Christabel asked.

The question was so innocently touching that Francis's heart twisted in anguish. He ignored her question and pulled her backpack off her shoulders before leading her into the kitchen for her dinner. As soon as he was satisfied that she would be occupied for a few minutes, Francis pulled Agnes into their bedroom and shut the door.

Agnes looked scared as she stood by the bed and patiently waited for Francis to start talking. Her fears however mounted when Francis continued to sigh heavily without uttering a word. Her hands grew clammy, and she twisted her fingers mercilessly.

"What's wrong, Kojo? You're scaring me," Agnes muttered.

Gently, Francis pulled her down to sit beside him on the bed. He knew how painful the news was going to be, and he didn't want her to slump to the floor when he eventually gathered the courage to talk. Her pregnancy was precious, and he was scared that she wouldn't be able to handle the news, and even worse, God forbid, lose the baby. He also knew that he couldn't keep the news to himself either. To say he felt torn was an understatement, and in his head, he cursed the universe for the bad timing.

"Aggie, promise me that you'll stay calm," Francis pleaded.

She did not say a word but got ready to brace herself. Francis cleared his throat. He knew that Agnes was only trying to put on a brave face. He could feel her hands trembling, which didn't make it any easier for him. The lump in his throat grew bigger and bigger until he was sure he would never swallow again.

"It's Eno Mmeraa. I got a call about an hour ago that she has passed," Francis spluttered.

Agnes's scream pierced through the air. She twisted away from Francis and slipped to the floor where she rolled and wailed. It broke Francis to see his wife so devastated, but there was nothing he could do at that moment to console her. The pain of losing a loved one could only be described as having been run over by a train and surviving to feel the pain. He knelt beside her and pulled her into his arms. Losing Eno Mmeraa was bad enough, but losing the baby too would be a pain he wouldn't even wish on his worst enemy.

For the rest of the evening, Agnes remained holed up in their bedroom while Francis catered to Christabel's needs. When he rejoined her after Christabel had gone to bed, he relaxed when he saw Agnes on the bed. However, she was so distraught and withdrawn that it looked like she had lost weight in the few hours since the news. Her dress was soaked through with tears, and her hair was a messy mass. Francis was astounded by what grief could do.

"I think we should go to the hospital for a check-up. You look too pale, and I don't like it considering your condition," Francis said.

"I'll be fine, Francis. Please. Don't worry," Agnes replied.

*　　*　　*

Agnes mourned her mother for weeks. Every night she cried herself to sleep, and every morning she woke with swollen eyes and a pounding head. The house was thick with sadness, almost suffocating. Even Christabel, too young to understand what had happened, sensed that something was wrong. She would often climb into her mother's lap and pat her face with her hands, as if she could wipe away the tears herself. Francis tried to hold things together, but each time he looked at Agnes his heart clenched. He wondered whether there would ever come a time when his family experienced constant happiness. Life always seemed to hand them joy with one hand and snatch it away with the other.

Agnes's grief was raw, but in her sorrow, her thoughts turned toward her sisters. It had been years since she had spoken to them properly. The bitterness of past betrayals had left deep cracks between them, and Francis had often warned her that some wounds were better left alone. But grief was not rational. The loss of their mother pushed her beyond reason. One evening, unable to bear the weight of silence any longer, she picked up the phone. The first call was to Afriyie. Her voice when she answered was soft but weary.

"Afriyie. It's me, Aggie," she said, her throat tightening.

There was a pause on the other end, then a sigh.

"I know. I heard… about Maame."

The two sisters spoke in halting sentences, their words stumbling over years of distance. They cried together, yet neither dared to go further. When the call ended, Agnes sat for a long time just staring at the receiver. They had spoken, yes, but nothing had changed. There would be no reunion with Afriyie, at least not now. The second call, however, led to something more. When Agnes dialled Adwoa's number, she braced herself for rejection. Instead, Adwoa answered with a gasp.

"Aggie? Is that really you?"

"Yes," Agnes whispered, tears spilling again. "I… I just needed to hear your voice. Maame's gone, Adwoa. She's gone."

Her sister's response was immediate. "Then come. Come and see me. It's been too long."

That invitation cracked open a door Agnes thought had long been sealed shut. Within days, she and Francis were on their way to Adwoa's home. Francis said little as they travelled, his jaw tight, his hands gripping his knees. He did not trust Adwoa or Afriyie, and the thought of exposing Agnes, pregnant and fragile, to more disappointment unsettled him. He also knew better than to oppose her outright.

*   *   *

When they arrived, Christabel clung shyly to her mother's thigh, her wide eyes taking in the unfamiliar surroundings. Then the door swung open, and three children tumbled out. It was Adwoa's brood. Their laughter was a rush of sound, their energy spilling over as they surrounded Christabel with curiosity and excitement.

"This is your cousin," Adwoa said, her voice trembling with both pride and guilt.

She pulled Agnes into a fierce embrace, and for the first time in months, Agnes felt warmth that wasn't shadowed by sorrow.

Christabel, after her initial hesitation, loosened her grip on Agnes and followed her cousins into the house. In no time, they were chasing each other around the house, their laughter ringing out like music. Agnes stood watching, her heart caught between grief for the mother she had lost and joy at seeing her daughter embraced by family. Francis, however, remained distant. He leaned against the doorway, arms folded, eyes watchful. The reunion made him uneasy. Old betrayals were not so easily forgotten, and while Agnes's heart was softening, his remained hardened.

Later that evening, when they were finally alone, he spoke. "Aggie, I don't trust this," he said quietly. "You know what's happened before. Don't let your grief cloud your judgment."

Agnes shook her head. "I need this, Kojo. I can't do this alone. I want Christabel to know her family. Even if you don't understand, please ... don't take this from me."

He looked at her closely then, saw the desperation in her eyes, and chose silence over argument. Though every instinct in him wanted to resist, he swallowed his protest. She was carrying their unborn child, grieving her mother, and clinging to the one bit of hope she had found. He would not be the one to crush it.

For Agnes, reconnecting with Adwoa was like a breath of fresh air. After that visit, they spoke over the phone nearly every day and late into the night, sharing memories of their mother, stories of their childhood, and plans for their futures. The bond was not perfect; too much had happened for that, but it was a start. For Agnes, that was enough.

As days turned into weeks, the sadness in The Oppong household eased slightly. Agnes laughed more, especially when recalling Christabel's adventures with her cousins. Pregnancy continued its steady course, the life growing inside her a reminder that even in loss, something new was gained.

Francis watched it all with a guarded heart. He wanted to be happy for her, and in many ways he was, but deep down he feared that trusting too much in people, even family, would only lead to more heartbreak. And so, he stayed close to Agnes, protective, wary, but staying out of her way on the matter.

29

The couple reached a significant milestone in July 1999 when the Home Office granted them indefinite leave to remain in the UK. The news came as a shock to Francis, who had long lowered his expectations. Even as he held the letter in his hands, he could barely believe what he had read.

What a long road it had been to get to that moment. Their immigration status had always been a shadow over all they did, but they had grown used to living with it. However, he was grateful that Asher had pushed him and Agnes to be decisive on this one thing. So, two years prior to becoming 'legal', Francis had finally agreed to seek proper legal advice. A young solicitor in South London, specialising in immigration law, had explained that while their situation was complicated, there was still a way to apply for permanent residence. Francis had already served his sentence, and because Agnes and Christabel were dependents, the family could petition under the rules that gave weight to 'family life' in the UK.

It hadn't been straightforward though; they had submitted piles of paperwork, proof of tenancy agreements, letters from Mr Lawson about Francis's employment, Christabel's school attendance, even testimonies from Asher and Ms Maggie vouching for Agnes's community ties. Each document was a reminder of how much of their lives had been built in Britain, and how much they had to lose if it all went wrong. The solicitor warned them that the process could take months, even years, but urged them to see it through.

Patience, however, was not Francis's strength. Every time a letter from the Home Office arrived, his heart sank in fear that it was a notice of deportation. Agnes, on the other hand, carried a quiet faith that things would eventually work out. Still, she never let her optimism rise too high, not after everything they had been through. It was no wonder then that when the letter of approval finally came through the letterbox, Francis was not at all ready for what it said. He read the letter once, twice, and a third time to make sure he had not misunderstood the contents. Could he dare believe that they no longer had to hide in the shadows? Agnes who had joined him for the second read also had doubts about what she had read. Her hands trembled as she reached for his.

"Francis... it's real. They've said yes."

Then she started to cry softly. For her, the approval represented security. She had carried the grief for her mother throughout her pregnancy, her tears often falling in silence as she folded tiny clothes for the baby on the way. Now, with the certainty of their status, she allowed herself to imagine raising two children in a place where the ground beneath her feet finally felt steady.

Christabel, though she had no idea what was going on, picked up on the joy buzzing in the house. To her, the letter simply meant that her parents were smiling again, and that the baby in Mummy's belly might arrive into a world less clouded by fear. "Will the baby sleep in my room?" she asked, her eyes shining. Agnes laughed, brushing her daughter's hair from her face. "We'll see, my princess. First, let's get the baby here safely."

Thankfully, the pregnancy was progressing well, despite Agnes's lingering grief. Her belly had blossomed, round and firm, and Christabel loved resting her head against it, talking to her sibling in singsong whispers. Francis would sometimes watch them quietly, torn between happiness and a dull ache in his chest. He knew Agnes still cried at night for her mother, and he felt powerless to stop her pain. Now with the Home Office's approval, he began to believe that life might still hold better days for them.

After the happy news, their flat felt lighter than it had in years. The approval didn't erase the hardships or the sadness, but it gave them something priceless: the chance to breathe. For the first time, Francis allowed himself to imagine a future in the UK that wasn't based on borrowed time. It was a future where Christabel could grow up without the shadow of deportation, where their unborn child could be born into stability, and where Agnes might finally find rest after so many years of turmoil.

* * *

As the summer sun poured through the thin curtains of their flat on the afternoon of 21 August 1999, Agnes, now at full term, felt a mixture of anticipation and dread. It was the day of her planned admission to give birth to their second child. In view of the difficulties with Christabel's birth, she was scheduled for another C-section. Francis, who had been restless all morning, paced the room as Agnes prepared for the hospital. Christabel, on the other hand was full of energy, and skipped around asking endless questions.

"Mummy, is the baby coming today? Can I see it first? Will the baby play with me right away?"

Agnes smiled faintly, resting her hand on her belly. "Patience, Christabel. Yes, your brother is coming today, but you won't be able to play with him yet."

Once Agnes was ready, they walked Christabel a few minutes down their road to a couple, Mr and Mrs Agyeman, that they had befriended. The family had agreed to keep Christabel until the baby's arrival. The Agyemans welcomed them warmly, promising to treat Christabel like their own. Christabel barely looked back as she ran inside to join their daughter Jacqueline. Both sets of parents laughed loudly at the excitement that bubbled out of the girls. After thanking the couple for the umpteenth time, Francis and Agnes called a taxi to take them to St George's for a second and hopefully happier delivery.

As soon as they announced their arrival at the maternity ward hospital, Agnes was prepared for theatre. It was an unusually quiet shift, and so in less than an hour after her admission, the midwife announced that it was her turn to get into theatre. As the porter wheeled her from her bed, across the ward, into the lift, and into theatre, memories of November 1991 floated back. She was making the exact same journey as she had done back then, but this time, she had Francis by her side. He held her hand tightly until he was asked to give room for Agnes to be prepared for the procedure. The midwife assured Francis that he would be able to join Agnes in theatre once he had gowned up and instructed on what to do.

There was much hustle and bustle as the doctors and midwives prepped Agnes, explaining every step. After what felt like an eternity, it was finally time to get baby out. That part went by so fast that neither had time to take in what actually happened. The doctor suddenly worked so swiftly that the next thing they heard was the piercing cry of a newborn punctuate the still air in the room. The midwife lifted a wriggling body into the air and announced, "It's a boy!"

Agnes burst into tears of relief and joy, and Francis felt a lump rise in his throat. He couldn't believe it when minutes later, he was handed his son who felt warm and fragile in his arms. He whispered a prayer under his breath, thanking God for this miracle that they named Elvis Oppong.

Just as it had been eight years earlier, Agnes and Elvis remained in hospital for a full five days. Having taken time off from work, Francis spent most days with them, and they were thankful that the Agyemans had insisted on keeping Christabel until mother and baby were back home. It gave Francis and Agnes time to share the experience they had not been able to the first time round; in fact they doubled the portion to make up for what they had missed with Christabel.

Agnes and Elvis were given the all clear to go home exactly on day five. They were eager for Christabel to meet Elvis, so as soon as the taxi dropped them at home, and Francis had settled them in, he rushed over to pick Christabel up. She greeted her father with an extra dose of her usual excitement, knowing that she was soon to meet her baby brother. Francis just about managed to thank his neighbours over Christabel's squeals of delight before rushing back to their flat. There Christabel burst through the door straight to her parents' bedroom where she knew the cot was waiting.

"He's so small!" she exclaimed, gently poking his blanket-wrapped hand through the bars. "I'm going to teach him everything. He's my best friend already." Her eyes sparkled with pride, and Francis and Agnes exchanged a glance that said that through all they had endured, their family was complete.

30

A few days later, Francis went into work briefly to sort out some paperwork. He hadn't expected to see anyone as he had gone in very early. However, Mr Lawson was already there.

"Francis, give me the good news," Mr Lawson said with a knowing grin.

Francis nodded. "Yes! Everything went smoothly. Agnes had a boy. I have a son."

Mr Lawson slapped him on the back. "Congratulations, Francis! Wait here. I have something for you."

He disappeared into his office and seconds later emerged with a large and neatly wrapped bundle.

"My lovely wife got a few things for the baby, and you can't say no," he said firmly. "Take them. And more importantly, take a few weeks off to look after your family. Send my congratulations to Agnes."

Francis was humbled. He'd not expected anything; he never did, but the generosity touched him deeply. He thanked Mr Lawson over and over, his voice almost breaking.

Back home, Agnes marvelled at the beautiful baby clothes, blankets and little shoes tucked inside the package from The Lawsons. She was so touched that on the spot, she clasped her hands together and whispered a prayer for them.

"May God bless Mr Lawson and his family a hundredfold."

* * *

The weeks that followed were filled with expected sleepless nights, feeding schedules, and endless nappy changes, but Agnes embraced them with newfound joy. Elvis's arrival had also dulled the pain of losing her mother, making it easier for her to embrace her new role of a mother of two. She sang softly to him, sometimes the same lullabies her mother had once sung to her. Though tears often slipped down her cheeks when she did, they were not just tears of despair. Francis also took to his elevated status of a father of two. In the evenings, he would cradle Elvis in his arms, his big hands dwarfing the tiny bundle, while Christabel snuggled beside him. Sometimes, Agnes just stood in the doorway, taking in the sight of her family together, the image she had once feared she might never see. For that toom she had a prayer.

"Thank you, Lord, for this second chance."

* * *

Soon it was Elvis's six-month milestone, and the family had adjusted perfectly to a new rhythm. Francis had since returned to work with a renewed sense of purpose, while Agnes mastered the balance of caring for both children. Christabel adapted beautifully, proudly declaring herself the 'helper of the house', fetching nappies and singing Elvis to sleep. The home, though small and cramped, overflowed with love. However, disruption was around the corner — it was time to move again ... and again ... and again ... and yet again. The Oppongs were now at the mercy of the beast that was London's housing system.

The first move came when Elvis was six months old in February 2000. Fortunately, it was still within Croydon. There was a little more to pack this time around. Whilst Francis was agitated by the timing, Agnes took it in her stride and reminded Francis to count their blessings. With that in mind, whenever Francis looked at Elvis, he was reminded that joy always came in the morning and after the darkest storms; when he listened to Christabel cooing over her brother, he was reminded that their dream of a family had come to life. For Agnes, what mattered was that they were a complete family, plus they had the security of having recognised legal status to be in the country.

The flat was modest, with two bedrooms and a small shared bathroom. However, the walls were thin, and every step from the neighbours above or next door echoed through into their flat and vice versa. One afternoon, Christabel, curious and restless, knocked over a lamp. The glass shattered across the wooden floor, leaving a mess of shards and fragments. Agnes, startled, quickly scooped Elvis up from the sofa and soothed him before she could sweep up the shards. Her nerves were also frayed especially as she worried about the neighbours. It was a small incident, but it was a symbol of how precarious life in temporary accommodation was. Spills, loud noises, and minor accidents were daily trials, but Agnes learned to juggle caring for her children while keeping them and herself safe.

* * *

The second move came about six months later, just after Elvis had turned one. This time they moved a little further out of Croydon to New Addington, where they stayed for eight months. The flat there was slightly larger, but some rooms remained bitterly cold during winter, and the kitchen facilities were minimal. Christabel had to change schools again, which frustrated her. She became quieter and more cautious, retreating into herself as the stress of constant change became too much. Elvis, by contrast, was fortunately a placid baby. He rarely cried for long periods, and even though he could pick up on the changes in his environment, it didn't seem to bother him. His nature offered a small but steadying presence for Agnes and Francis. Through that second change, Agnes's confidence to create a balance and harmony grew; she was particularly focused on being present for Christabel as she navigated the constant changes.

* * *

By late 2001, The Oppongs had moved a third time, back to Croydon, just off Davidson Road. They remained there for just over a year, and though the house was a moderate size, the neighbourhood was noisy. Agnes poured her energy into maintaining some stability, and to do that, she made a decision to continue as a housewife and focus on the children. Francis continued working hard, grateful for Mr Lawson's steady support. Still, the pressure that came with constantly uprooting a family at the drop of a hat could not be avoided. Christabel had attended three primary schools in three years and had grown wary of making new friends. She was now a shy girl who was easily frustrated, but Agnes did her best to create routines that anchored her daughter in a world that was constantly shifting.

* * *

Finally, in 2003, the council found them a permanent home, a lovely three-bedroom house in Thornton Heath. It was in a quiet residential area, had a large garden where Christabel and Elvis could run freely and a driveway. The house itself felt solid, stable and welcoming in a way that the temporary flats never had. Agnes could now dedicate herself fully to her family without the looming anxiety of being uprooted again, while Francis could focus on providing for his family without fear of losing their home. Christabel flourished at her new school, slowly forming lasting friendships, while Elvis grew steadily, healthy and cheerful.

Those three years had tested them in ways they never could have imagined. Yet through it all, they had come out the other end intact. They had mastered the art of finding joy in simple, everyday routines: quiet evenings together, family mealtimes, playtime in the garden — all comforting rhythms of family life. Francis took pride in watching his children grow, even as he quietly reflected on the upheaval they had endured. Agnes, resilient and determined, had held the household together, balancing care for her children with nurturing her marriage.

Even as life settled into a steady and predictable rhythm, the lessons of the past remained. The memory of uncertainty lingered, reminding them that nothing in life was guaranteed. Yet, for the first time in years, they could breathe easy, knowing that they had each other, and that their family, tested by hardship and strengthened by love, was finally whole. Their journey, though far from over, had brought them to a place of hope and quiet triumph. These were not the things they had set out to achieve when they had first landed in London all those years ago; they had turned out to be far greater and more valuable than they could ever have imagined. These were the foundations and pillars that would hold them up when faced with the new challenges and adventures that awaited them in their future. In the meantime, they could rest assured that this chapter of their lives had ended with much having been accomplished, the seeds for a great legacy sown, and the comfort and security of finally finding and creating a place to call home.

ABOUT THE AUTHOR

Christabel Oppong is a British-Ghanaian writer, storyteller, and advocate whose debut memoir, *The Unspoken Truth: You Never Know Your Tomorrow*, draws from her family's real-life journey of migration, love, loss, and survival. Her emotionally raw TikTok series sharing this story went viral, amassing over 5 million views and resonating with audiences across the world.

Raised in South London, Christabel weaves her powerful personal journey with rich Ghanaian culture, giving readers a deeply emotional and culturally rooted story.

Her writing is a tribute to her late parents, whose strength and suffering shaped the narrative she now shares.

Beyond writing, Christabel is a wife and a mother of three. She is passionate about helping others feel seen, heard, and understood through honest storytelling.

Conscious Dreams
PUBLISHING

Transforming diverse writers
into successful published authors

www.consciousdreamspublishing.com

authors@consciousdreamspublishing.com

Let's connect

www.ingramcontent.com/pod-product-compliance
Lightning Source LLC
Chambersburg PA
CBHW030304080526
44584CB00012B/437